WILLIAM FAULKNER: *An Interpretation*

WILLIAM FAULKNER

AN INTERPRETATION

by IRVING MALIN

GORDIAN PRESS
NEW YORK
1972

Originally Published 1957
Reprinted 1972

Library of Congress Catalog Card Number — 76-165664
ISBN — 87752-154-9

For my wife Ruth
who understands why

r

PREFACE

In his review of *The Portable Faulkner* Robert Penn Warren suggests that we should study isolated incidents to discover the importance of compulsion and will in the work of Faulkner. But I believe that the themes of rigidity (compulsion) as a personal and social evil and the need to rebel against rigidity in order to gain freedom (will) are so important to Faulkner that he chooses to concretize them in the myth of father and son. The "images" Warren mentions are, in a real sense, the underlying principles of structure in the major novels.

I investigate certain related problems which have, for the most part, been neglected—for instance, Faulkner's characterization of women, and his use of the Bible. I consider both Freud and Jung because they are concerned not only with myth, but with the need to grow up, to adjust to the ever-increasing anguish of our contemporary world. I try to indicate that Faulkner can hunt—to use one of his favorite words—for the solution to his own psychological problems and, in turn, to those of Darl Bundren, Joe Christmas, or Charles Mallison Jr. Thus the plan of the book.

This book could not have been written without the aid of three of my teachers. I wish to thank especially Charles A. Allen of Stanford University, Richard Scowcroft, also of Stanford, and Charles Child Walcutt of Queens College for their answers to my frantic questions. My debt to my wife can be acknowledged at this time, but never discharged.

I also want to express my gratitude to the following for permission to quote copyrighted material:

To Liveright Publishing Corporation, for quotations from *Soldiers' Pay*, by William Faulkner (copyright R 1953 William Faulkner, permission of Liveright Publishers, New

York), and from *Mosquitoes*, by William Faulkner (copyright R 1954, William Faulkner, permission of Liveright Publishers, New York).

To Random House, Inc., for quotations from *Absalom, Absalom! A Fable, As I Lay Dying, Collected Stories of William Faulkner, Go Down, Moses and Other Stories, The Hamlet, Intruder in the Dust, Light in August, Requiem for a Nun, Sanctuary, The Sound and the Fury,* and *The Wild Palms,* by William Faulkner; and from *Great Voices of the Reformation,* edited by Harry Emerson Fosdick.

Also to the following: Cornell University Press, *Ancient Israel,* by Harry Orlinsky; *Critique* (formerly *Faulkner Studies*), *Mirrors of Chartres Street,* by William Faulkner; Dodd, Mead & Company, *Psychology of the Unconscious,* by C. G. Jung (copyright © 1916, 1944, by Beatrice M. Hinkle); The Hogarth Press Ltd., *Civilization and Its Discontents* and *Collected Papers,* V, by Sigmund Freud; *The Kenyon Review,* "The Stone and the Crucifixion: Faulkner's *Light in August*," by Richard Chase, and "The Hero in the New World: William Faulkner's 'The Bear,' " by R. W. B. Lewis; *New Republic,* "Cowley's Faulkner," by Robert Penn Warren; W. W. Norton & Company, Inc., *The Psychoanalytic Theory of Neurosis,* by Otto Fenichel; Pantheon Books Inc., *Two Essays on Analytical Psychology* (Bollingen Series), by C. G. Jung; Penguin Books Ltd., *An Introduction to the Bible,* by Stanley Cook; Rinehart & Company, Inc., *Escape from Freedom,* by Erich Fromm; Routledge and Kegan Paul Ltd., *Totem and Taboo,* by Sigmund Freud; Mark Schorer, "Technique as Discovery"; The Times-Picayune Publishing Co., "Out of Nazareth" (reprinted in *Mirrors of Chartres Street*), by William Faulkner; and Yale University Press, *The Psychology of Jung,* by Jolan Jacobi.

IRVING MALIN

STANFORD UNIVERSITY

CONTENTS

THE THEME OF RIGIDITY

THE THEME OF RIGIDITY

What does the theme of rigidity mean? Or, more specifically, what kinds of rigidity are the novels of Faulkner concerned with? It seems to me that like Proust and Joyce he is an investigator of the psychological condition of his characters. He tries to understand and to present the principles which govern motivation, learning, and memory. By studying his psychology we can learn about the fundamental aspects of his theme of rigidity.

Faulkner believes that the individual often refuses to come to terms with the disorder of our contemporary world; that he tries to flee by adopting an inflexible pattern of behavior which offers solace in certainty of responses. Faulkner calls the pattern which orders personal existence in basically rigid ways, the compulsive plan, the "design." This design for living can be sought consciously or unconsciously. In his novels the major characters adopt the pattern either in an intellectually conceived or in a subconsciously desired way. A man's design is rigid because he constantly notices and yields to his own needs for self-preservation and security. Faulkner apparently believes that because the personal design is made in the absence of psychological strength it can only lose whatever constructive value it could have as order. In spite of the potentialities he has for adjustment, integration, and completion a man becomes a "demon"—Faulkner's term—because he loses his will as his design assumes an overwhelming influence. Like Sutpen in *Absalom, Absalom!* he then discovers "not what he had wanted to do but what he just had to do whether he has wanted to or not, because if he did not do it he knew that he could never live with himself for the rest of his life." The design becomes a burden which the individual carries without an awareness of his lost freedom.

In *Light in August* we have an example in Hightower of a deliberate attempt to adopt rigidity and to live with it. The Reverend Mr. Hightower lives in seclusion, in a house so hidden that "the light from the corner street lamp scarcely touches it." He learns of events in the community through conversations with only one person, Byron Bunch. It is significant that we always see him at the window as twilight approaches, because he is more interested in reverie than in contact with other people. Faulkner shows us that the Reverend's behavior is the result of a personal design which he developed in his youth. His childhood is dominated by the sickness of his mother and the absence of parental love even from his father, who is a preacher. It seems to Hightower that the tales of the Negro cook about his grandfather who fought and died in the Civil War are able to offer insights into action. He believes that he can relive the war experiences of the general, which are more alive to him than the sick atmosphere of his household. He reflects so much upon these past glories that he can become, as it were, a "single instant of darkness in which a horse [his grandfather's] galloped and a gun crashed." Hightower decides that he will marry because his future wife, the daughter of a church official, can help him obtain a position as preacher in Jefferson near where his grandfather was killed. He does not consider her individual need for affection. This personal design is a substitute for married love, and the inadequacy of the Reverend (real and symbolic) forces her to become promiscuous in her effort to gain satisfaction. Her suicide—she jumps from a hotel window in Memphis—enters the consciousness of Hightower only as he sits in final seclusion at the window of his house. He is a ghost because he has tried to become his grandfather in spite of the fact that he had his own life to lead.

In *As I Lay Dying* Addie Bundren learns as a child from her father that living is not easy, "that the reason for living was to get ready to stay dead." The emphasis upon the uncertainty and insecurity of life is never to leave her mind. At first, Addie cannot accept the words of her father, and she rebels in a symbolic way by marrying Anse, a weak and unsuspecting man who can satisfy her self-assertive needs. But marriage also involves chance. Addie discovers that occasionally children are born at unexpected times, and she feels threatened. Once more she recalls the words of her father when life has tricked her. The birth of Darl forces Addie to adopt a pattern of behavior which stresses the acceptance of and the preparation for death. She forgets about life in the careful way the Reverend Mr. Hightower does; she accepts only those needs of her children which pertain to her desire to lie calmly, "getting ready to clean [her] house" in order to end terrible living. She can call Jewel her child because he is born after the formation of her pattern. While she nurses him he represents the loss of the violence of life, and the discovery of the silence of death. Indeed, Faulkner means to suggest by his title that Addie not only is on her deathbed as the novel opens, but, in a symbolic sense, has been there since the time Darl and her conscious design were born.

Some of Faulkner's characters acquire the design in less conscious ways. In *Light in August* Percy Grimm acts like a soldier in peacetime. He organizes a militia in his community to see that the violators of the laws of the United States of America are captured and destroyed. He glorifies violence as self-preservation in the midst of active opposition. Faulkner shows us that Grimm wants to accept military discipline as the center of a design because he is unconsciously aware of the weakness of his own ego. He loses the need to define true selfhood in the ranks of the organization. He does not take time to think about self-realization because he concerns himself more and more with self-destruction. His demonstrations of military power hide a repressed but tremendous desire to inflict punishment upon other people and himself. Faulkner believes that Grimm's design is perhaps more dangerous than those of Hightower and Addie Bundren. It is more easily accepted by the community—it is not thought of as eccentric or asocial—because it can be glamorized as the law of the land. Other citizens admire the "burden which he now carried as light and weightless as his insignatory brass: a sublime and implicit faith in physical courage and blind obedience." The irony is that the externalization of rigidity in military organization can not only hide the burden of his design—it can even help him to achieve a kind of heroism in modern times.

Popeye in *Sanctuary*, like Percy Grimm, lives according to an unconscious pattern of rigidity. We know more about his childhood than about Grimm's, but I think that we can assume the two act because of corresponding motives. As a child Popeye learns that most people in the world are not to be trusted or respected in any way. His own father flees from his dazed mother; his grandmother, in an act of insanity, sets fire to the house in which he lives; his mother never recovers from "hard work and the lack of fresh air, diversion, and the disease [syphilis], the legacy which her brief husband had left her . . ." Popeye is tormented by this legacy of inherited disease coupled with environmental influences. He has no hair until he is five years old; he eats food specifically designed to help him gain weight; he lives in an institution of sorts. Early in his life Popeye, like Addie, learns that "living is terrible," and he believes that he has to rebel against his violent existence by acts of violence. He sees himself, in a sense, as an inhuman object which must destroy living things. Faulkner seems to believe that Popeye's childhood act of cutting up two birds is repeated in a compulsive manner. When he rapes Temple Drake with the corncob, he is again acting out the childhood incident, because in his manhood he is still an impotent criminal who feels inwardly that he can achieve security only through violence. He cannot clean house for death as Addie and Hightower do; he must destroy daily to punish both himself and other people. What Faulkner is saying ironically is that although the community thinks of the militia leader, Grimm, as lawgiver, and the criminal, Popeye, as lawbreaker, their patterns are basically the same.

It is evident to those readers who are acquainted with contemporary psychology that Faulkner's investigation of the designs of these characters is in accord with many case histories. Erich Fromm tries to account for the same illusion of individuality in his *Escape from Freedom.* He believes that "instrumentalized" culture fosters the tendency to escape into compulsive patterning "in the process of which the isolated individual becomes an automaton, loses his self, and yet at the same time consciously conceives of himself as free and subject only to himself."[1] As children we are taught to suppress our emotions. We are told that we should not hate people, or that we should not feel ill. This continual suppres-

---

[1] Erich Fromm, *Escape from Freedom* (New York: Farrar and Rinehart, 1941), p. 241.

sion can lead to hostility, which is hidden for a while, but which eventually directs itself against other people or the already ineffectual ego. So Grimm must join a military organization, Popeye must kill people, and Hightower must torment himself through reverie. It is the failure to recognize the significance of feeling (the failure D. H. Lawrence attacked so passionately), to enjoy a balanced existence, which is responsible for the fact that Faulkner's characters, like Fromm's patients, submit to a new kind of authority and live as they do, unrelated to the world about them.

But Faulkner does not consider the design to be important merely because it is the outgrowth of a pathological condition. He does not delight in horror and disease. His concern with the design is important to us because he can relate the pattern of compulsion not only to a prevalent pathological condition in our times, but also to his own environment as a Southerner. He works outward from isolated examples such as Grimm, Hightower, Addie Bundren, and Popeye to see the total social implications of the desire for rigidity of existence. His own region, he believes, is grounded upon ideals as abstract and inhuman as the personal design. His novels suggest that the organization of the social and religious systems of the South resembles personal compulsion in that it does not allow individual Southerners to realize their own potentialities for human completion. From the typical attitude of white Southerners toward the Negro and toward the Calvinist faith, Faulkner would apparently have us conclude that many "normal" Southerners are just as pathological as a Hightower, or perhaps even that the region's social systems are accepted only by the mentally unbalanced.

The rigidity of the ante-bellum social organization is seen in *Absalom, Absalom!* Thomas Sutpen is one of the new citizens of the old South, and his life is dominated by the design to gain individual recognition through material conformity (in the same way that a man can now gain recognition if he is able to purchase and display the same goods as his neighbor). He is able to achieve his position of plantation owner through an abundance of courage and shrewdness. His courage is shown in the West Indies incident, at which time he enables a colonist's family to repel an attack by unfriendly natives. His shrewdness is demonstrated in his choice of a wife, who is a member of one of the most eminent and most respected families in Mississippi. Faulkner clearly suggests that Sutpen's personal compulsions are an important parallel to the social order. In his time slavery was the center of the Southern society. The plantation owner could gain the wealth he wanted through his exploitation of the Negro, who carried the taint of inferior status. Color was the mark of social distinction. The white man was not able to individualize any Negro because he could only consider him an abstraction, an object which picked cotton, something necessary for the execution of his plan. Faulkner believes that the idea of slavery became so dominant in the South that the plantation owners like Sutpen could not realize—or even take the time to consider—the basic inhumanity of slavery, even after the War ended. In the novel Sutpen does not seem to realize the overwhelming significance of the Northern victory. He tries to rebuild his fallen empire in the same way that he did before, and to hand down his ideas about slavery and the need for social rigidity to his white son. He wants to make his son accept his design and therefore to perpetuate concepts which were, in reality, responsible for the War and the material decay of Southern culture. All that Thomas Sutpen can say about his design is:

. . . You see, I had a design in mind. Whether it was a good or bad design is beside the point, the question is, where did I make the mistake in it, whom or what injure by it to the extent which this would indicate.

In his later novels, such as *Intruder in the Dust*, Faulkner seems to be saying that the North did not break down the rigid order of the past. Certainly there was the abolition of slavery and the proclamation of equality for all men. But the atmosphere of the new South is tense with the memory of the ante-bellum pattern of men like Sutpen (which was constructive in some ways) and the violence of a new disorderly existence. The Negro is now a "slave" because he is regarded as a more dangerous kind of abstraction than the one implied in past slavery. The Southerner can look at him as the cause of the War and the havoc of Reconstruction. He assumes that the Negro—not slavery—is the curse on the land, and any corruption that comes from a solitary black man is used as evidence of the corruption of the whole race. Crimes are committed by *Negro*. Every Southerner who preaches white supremacy acknowledges the need of a return to the old rigidity. His voice and the organization of the Ku Klux Klan prove that the problem Faulkner is concerned with is not an insignificant condition in our times. It has the regularity of common occurrence.

The conflict between Lucas Beauchamp and the community in *Intruder in the Dust* arises out of the fact that, although colored, he refuses to act like a Negro. Lucas does not consider himself part of the white man's abstraction of him and his race. He carries a gold toothpick in his mouth to symbolize his actual bond with the aristocratic Edmonds family. His way of dressing, of walking, of speaking, proclaims him as an oddity in the region. What is to be done with such an "uppity" Negro, the community asks. The answer, it seems, is to be found in lynching because Lucas Beauchamp is discovered one day standing next to the body of a white man. It does not matter whether he is innocent or guilty. Every Negro is, of course, guilty because he carries the taint of inferior status and sin. The boy hero, Charles Mallison Jr., can only feel the same as his seniors when he hears the news. He is too close to his environment to respond in any other way than to think immediately that Lucas is "just a nigger" in spite of all his aristocratic airs.

Miscegenation occupies an important place in the Faulkner novels. It inspires the wrath of the white man, because he believes that it can destroy the Southern social organization. The mixture of bloods symbolizes the permanent violation of distinctions between black and white. Color can no longer be a standard. The Negro can consider miscegenation a valid means of revenge because it proves without a doubt that the blood relationship of black to white is real and significant. If he cannot gain any recognition from white men, he will, he believes, force them to realize the inadequacies of their views of social rigidity by transmuting his black blood into the blood stream of the region. This definite mixture will symbolize the absence of any kind of social rigidity in future ages. In *Absalom, Absalom!* Thomas Sutpen is more afraid of miscegenation than he is of the possible incest between his daughter and Bon. He communicates his vision of horror to his white son. Even this son, Henry (who admires the sophistication of Bon, his black brother), trembles as he thinks about the social consequences of miscegenation. The scene of the murder of Bon by Henry after he has learned that the other is part black is a significant archetypal situation in Southern history.

Faulkner is also concerned with the rigidity of Calvinism. In his novels he seems to brood upon the Southerner's need to adopt the harshness of Protestant theology and to use it in order to justify his own awkward efforts to escape from the disorder of our times. Many men in their personal designs for security act and feel as if they belong to the select group of believers who are "saved." They easily assume indignant attitudes. They regard others not as individuals to be pitied or loved, but as infidels to be crucified, and they gain pleasure from crucifying them. Faulkner finds the Calvinist faith just as destructive as the physical violence of a Grimm. He believes that the warmth faith can bring, the needs of the spirit, are too easily forgotten by the Calvinist, who associates faith with his conviction of righteousness:

> For we are said to be justified through faith not in the sense however, that we receive within us any righteousness, but because the righteousness of Christ is credited to us, entirely as if it were ours, while our iniquity is not charged to us, so that one can truly call this righteousness simply the remission of sins.[2]

In *Light in August*, one significant attitude toward Calvinism is revealed in the characterization of McEachern. McEachern, the black-suited farmer, has a harshness of spirit and a self-righteousness which enable him to set his mind on things higher than the "lechery" he sees before him. His design is the need to teach his fellow men the glory of work and the love of the Lord. He does not completely believe in the goodness of men; his exercises of conversion are dominated by compulsion rather than by the warmth of hope and faith. His faith is merely the "rigid abnegation of all compromise." The irony is evident in the brutal description of the Sabbath on which McEachern decides to teach the catechism to his adopted son. Force is his method of instruction. He observes the clock because his torture is methodical like his working habits, and because he does not (of course)

2 John Calvin, "From Instructions in Faith," in *Great Voices of the Reformation*, ed. Harry Emerson Fosdick (New York: Random House, 1952), p. 226.

want to miss the church service. The prayer he offers is not one of spiritual dedication or promise, but a business arrangement which emphasizes the need for submission to absolutism—a curious externalization of his own weakness and self-righteousness. His adherence to Protestant theology is an outlet for his own hatred of humanity. He can follow the Law and construct his personal design about it because it is as cold and abstract as his daily routine. This association is significant. It is also realized by Hightower at the end of the novel when he begins to see the inadequacies of his own design. The doom of mankind is part of the pleasure Protestantism affords. Believers submit to absolute Law, and this submission prevents them from being part of life because they do not enjoy any "peace in which to sin and to be forgiven." They occasionally discover that they must assert their own sense of freedom, but they act then without restraint and knowledge. Hightower thinks:

Pleasure, ecstasy, they cannot seem to bear: their escape from it is in violence, in drinking and fighting and praying; catastrophe too, the violence identical and apparently inescapable *And so why should not their religion drive them to crucifixion of themselves and one another?*

The attitude of Faulkner toward the Calvinist faith can also be seen in comments in his other novels. In *The Wild Palms* the doctor and his wife who rent the cottage to the unmarried couple, Harry and Charlotte, are also representative of self-righteous indignation toward sinners. They have never come to terms with their own sexuality, have repressed it, and so they condemn Harry and Charlotte not for their illicit union so much as for the fact of their ever-present conscious sexuality. But Faulkner believes that they do not express their disfavor (especially as they are receiving money from the two sinners). Indeed, they show hospitality by offering assistance and gifts to Harry and Charlotte to show that they *do* love their un-Christian neighbors. Even their actions in this respect are meaningless. The feeling of charity is absent and the bowl of soup, which they offer to the couple, becomes a symbol of "the uncompromising Christian deed performed not with sincerity or pity but through duty." It is perhaps enlightening to see the assertion of Faulkner's attitude toward Calvinism in *Intruder in the Dust,* which, for the most part, concerns social rigidity. It is not embodied in characterization as it is in McEachern or the doctor, but it can be seen in the comment made during the graveyard scene. The boy, Charles, and his uncle have come to investigate the disappearance of Gowrie's corpse and the substitution of the corpse of Jake Montgomery. For a moment Charles forgets about the innocence of Lucas. He looks up at the church steeple in a sudden kind of illumination, almost a Joycean epiphany, before they can begin to uncover the earth. Faulkner writes, "he remembered the tall slender spires which said Peace and the squatter utilitarian belfries which said Repent and he remembered one which even said Beware but this one said simply: Burn."

Faulkner believes that the Calvinist must have opposing views in regard to the Father and the Son. The spiritual striving of the individual is seen in a glorified context in the image of the Son on the cross. But the Calvinist cannot pity Christ or understand the reasons for his spiritual wounds. He sees only his own desire for self-immolation, for death, in the wounds of the Son who lost his life so that Man could live and love. Faulkner believes that the Calvinist has more respect for the Father because He is more just and masculine than His crucified Son. He embodies the principle of the "Shalt Not"—to use Faulkner's term. He is the Law to be followed in the presence of ruthless methods of enforcement by men like Calvin. Faulkner shows us that the worship of the Lord of Calvin forces men to accept with religious fervor rigidity of an organized set of doctrines parallel in rigidity to the rigidity of the personal patterns of Hightower and Addie Bundren. It is clear that he is afraid of the establishment of another Geneva in the new world.

It is worth noting that Faulkner uses the symbol of war to emphasize his theme of the rigidity of Calvinism. In *A Fable* the commander of the group of soldiers that mutinied is held responsible for their mutiny, although he had nothing to do with it. The absolutism of Law is dominant in wartime. Faulkner believes that war becomes a monstrous compulsion which destroys soldiers and civilians, those who favor war and those who oppose it. The Corporal in the novel represents Christ on the cross. His martyrdom is the result of his need to assert pacifism and humility during the war. He believes that his act of mutiny can countermand the rigidity of war and, indeed, make "even ruthless and all-powerful and unchallengeable Authority . . . impotent before that massed unresisting undemanding passivity." One of the lessons of this fable is that too many men submit to rigidity (be it religious or military or psychological), because it is much easier, as Dostoyevsky wrote in his tale of the Grand Inquisitor, to gain security in the loss of one's self in some external authority which, the individual believes, is more powerful than his own "insignificant" ego. Faulkner ironically suggests in the novel that rebellion against authority in our society is not only defeated—it is made to appear as rigidity. I believe that this is the meaning of the end. The corpse of this Corporal who fought for peace is buried, by chance occurrence, to symbolize the Unknown Soldier.

Actually Faulkner is saying that the present time is one of meaningless movement for anyone who is uncertain. Such a person is enabled to escape from facing the present by his rigid adherence to the past. He does not use his knowledge of the past to interpret and evaluate the present; he sees the past as too glorious to be considered part of a continuum which embraces all life experience. The uncertain man can easily admire the active lives of men who were stronger than himself, because their lives offer him the certainty he seeks. He repeatedly discovers meanings in the past which may never have existed. The danger is, of course, increased if the traditions of the past did have same kind of greatness of action, some kind of constructive value. Faulkner believes that the reasonable balance necessary for the critical evaluation of history can easily disappear for the Southerner who feels that his ante-bellum South was an isolated Eden. He wants to gain a fixity in history only because of his driving need to find some sort of temporal rigidity which offers the feeling of security.

The romantic conception of the pre-War South is apparent in *Sartoris*. The Sartoris family is so conscious of the memory of John Sartoris that his presence is as "palpable" as that of a living person. His virile spirit haunts the household in the form of his Civil War sabers which are locked in the attic and the piano in the living room at which he occasionally sat. Perhaps the tales about him are important in this respect: they serve to instill in listeners a sense of the grandeur and power and beauty of the old order. The tales about Sartoris are full of blood and thunder and are neither heard nor interpreted rationally by Old Colonel Bayard, his son; Young Bayard, his grandson; or Simon, the Negro servant. Faulkner believes that these characters cannot come to terms with present conditions because they do not understand both the potentialities and limitations of their heritage. Their vision of the past is as overromanticized as the tales of Aunt Jenny Du Pre. Even Aunt Jenny, though she senses the association of doom with the Sartoris family, is totally attracted to the exploits of John Sartoris, who captured Northerners in the Civil War, constructed a railway to the North, ran for legislature, and eventually died in a duel. Faulkner describes one of her tales, a sentimental vision of Southern aristocrats: it is a gallant and tragic portrayal of two wild boys who take on the aspect of angels and save the entire South from destruction by the satanic North.

Throughout his novels Faulkner shows that the weak man is a victim of paradox, that he tries to fit his view of history into his personal design because of his inbred failure to face the present. But this attempt is more than any man can make. A design leads only to a destructive existence. Faulkner shows us that the inability of the individual to accept temporal change is a result of the failure to integrate past and present experiences into the meaningful order of life.

In *Light in August* Grimm lives "dissociated from mechanical time." He realizes inwardly that he cannot face the stress of his own age; he convinces himself, however, that he is the victim of "having been born not alone too late but not late enough to have escaped first hand knowledge of the lost time when he should have been a man instead of a child." The actions of Grimm would ordinarily be considered insane. But he can never gain the clear perspective necessary for a new evaluation of past events because of his obedience to his design, and because his views on the war are not considered by other people to be the outgrowth of an abnormal condition. His vision of the past is not in real conflict with the violent "peacetime" of his own age. The eyes of Hightower are turned in a backward glance to the glorious death of his grandfather. His view of this remote event has become so much a part of him that "it is as though out of his sub-

conscious he produces without volition the few crystalliza-
tions of stated instances by which his own dead life in the
actual world had been governed and ordered once." His
madness is emphasized by Faulkner's description of the
actual death of the general. The general was not killed in
battle; on the contrary, his death was the result of an attempt
to steal chickens from a backyard henhouse. A woman—and,
as if this were not sufficient irony, "likely enough the wife of
a Confederate soldier"—shot him. Yet the design of the
Reverend Mr. Hightower permits him to add mystery to
the circumstances until the entire situation gains the appearance of a kind of grotesque miracle.

In *Requiem for a Nun* Temple has not come to terms with
the present because she clings to an inflexible pattern of
behavior. She does not realize that her experiences in the
past—being raped by the impotent Popeye, living in a
Memphis brothel—have remained dormant in her mind. She
tries to begin a new life not as Temple Drake of the past but
as Mrs. Gowan Stevens of the present. She has two children
who are cared for by Nancy, a Negress and a former slut.
It is not the maid who is responsible, as the jury and the
townspeople believe, for the murder of Temple's youngest
child—it is the mother herself. She accepts the advances of
a blackmailer because he represents to her his lustful brother
Red (to whom she was once attracted) and the Memphis
underworld associations of her own past. This is the cause
of family tragedy because Nancy believes that it is, perhaps,
more virtuous to strangle the child than to permit Temple
and the criminal to flee with it. Gavin Stevens, the uncle who
is the spokesman for Faulkner, again and again emphasizes
the thought to Temple:

. . . everyone—must, or may have to, pay . . . the past; that
past is something like a promissory note with a trick clause in it,
which, as long as nothing goes wrong, can be manipulated in an
orderly manner, but which fate or luck or chance can foreclose on
you without warning.

Afraid of the truth of his view, of the failure of her entire
life, Mrs. Gowan Stevens exclaims impatiently at another
point in the novel: "Temple Drake is dead." Her uncle looks
at her and answers: "The past is never dead. It's not even
past."

In all his novels Faulkner is saying with violence that the individual in our times frequently *does not* want to explore the causes of being. An understanding of his situation requires a correct vision of the "image of compulsion." The horror of the situation lies, for Faulkner, in the fact that people have neither the strength nor the insight necessary to relieve themselves of their burden. A person with a design cannot change because he cannot part with whatever value his design can offer. He is doomed. Occasionally he knows it. But it is wrong to assert that Faulkner's art rebels against civilization. His novels rebel against those patterns which equate rigidity with order and do not permit a man to prove that he has the strength to stand alone, without fear and trembling.

THE FATHER-SON MYTH

2

THE FATHER-SON MYTH

William Faulkner's great-grandfather was a legend during the writer's youth. Colonel Falkner became, in a way, the hero of Faulkner's first novel dealing with Yoknapatawpha County, *Sartoris*. Here we can see that, just as Faulkner's great-grandfather lived in his native region although dead, John Sartoris, also dead, occupies a unique position in the life of his family and the town. His deeds are legendary and are not questioned. They are accepted—whether good or bad—because they seem to embody a curious mixture of violence, commercial enterprise, and Southern gentility. We feel that the Sartoris family still lives in the present according to the heroic conception of this ancestor. Colonel Bayard refuses to ride in a car because he believes that his father would never do so; Simon, the aged Negro servant, recounts the glory of past skirmishes in which Sartoris participated; the objects which belong to the ancestor, even his tombstone, are worshiped. The opening of the novel is important in this respect; we learn here that John Sartoris' ghost accompanies old man Falls as he visits Sartoris' son, Old Bayard. This ghostly presence is not unusual—as we shall see—because John Sartoris represents the first and almost perfect father image in Faulkner's novels. But even in this novel we receive a sense of uneasiness when we read about young Bayard Sartoris, the grandson. Bayard does not seem to belong to this aristocratic family. He races cars as he raced planes during World War I; he cannot sit in the house, cannot accept the same environment in which John Sartoris lived. His actions are chaotic and self-destructive. The other members of the family are unable to understand the motives for these actions, and they do not realize that he is troubled by war injuries and some deeper trauma. After Bayard wrecks the car, giving his father a heart attack, he lies in his bed thinking that he cannot tolerate the idea of living until his seventieth birthday. (He is only twenty-six.) Bayard does finally reach the end in a faulty airplane which he volunteers to pilot for a corrupt businessman. The plane disintegrates in midair as if to answer his prayers. In his desire to rebel against an unknown cause and to destroy himself, Bayard is the first representation of the son in the novels of Faulkner. *Sartoris* then is a starting point for myth, but the figures are indistinct and do not meet in conflict.

I believe that after he finished this early novel Faulkner realized that he had expressed some ideas which troubled him. He understood before he could put into words the flaws in the way John Sartoris lived, that Bayard was obsessed with an inherited sense of doom. Before he was able to write his other novels Faulkner had to conceptualize consciously the real inadequacies of the ante-bellum code and the need to rebel against this code. He did so before *The Sound and the Fury.* He believed that he could concrete his themes of the rigidity of personal compulsion and social organization through the use of the father image. He believed that he could symbolize the rebellion against environmental evils, the quest for new values, through his use of the son. In the novels before 1929, the only affectionate bond between the father and the son exists in childhood. But it seems as if this bond is broken as soon as the son begins to question his place in the household and in the world at large. The son recognizes the fact that his father refuses to consider his personal doubts. The father is too intent upon his own compulsive behavior to take the time to look at any problems which, he believes, do not pertain to his own design. The ensuing conflict is so dominant a pattern in Faulkner's work that it assumes a crucial place in his myth.

The conflict between the father and the son is apparent in *The Sound and the Fury.* Mr. Compson is not a heroic figure like John Sartoris; on the contrary, he is basically unglamorous. He lives intellectually according to an inflexible pattern which permits him to sit all day drinking, reading Horace and Livy, and writing bitter elegies about his fellow townspeople. Mr. Compson is resolute because of his desire to believe that life in the new South (and, indeed, all life) is so grotesque and tedious at the same time that a man is fortunate if he can escape from it. Neverthe-

less this belief in his own escape is folly for him. Mr. Compson thinks that men are limited not only by time and space
but also by the inability to realize their own stupidity and
weakness. "Because no battle is ever won he said. They're
not even fought. The field only reveals to man his own folly
and despair, and victory is an illusion of philosophers and
fools." Mr. Compson is both philosopher and fool because
he does not even believe in victory—only defeat. Of course,
there cannot be any set of traditional beliefs which stress the
potentialities of men to survive and to better themselves.
The meanings of sin and salvation do not exist. Christ is
envisioned by the father as a mortal who—like all other
mortals—"is worn away by a minute clicking of little wheels."
Mr. Compson cannot pity Christ's wounds or any wounds
because he cannot accept the conditions which govern life;
he does not want to remain alive in an alien world. Unfortunately, he cannot find contentment in his dipsomania. The
horror of the situation is that Mr. Compson discovers delight
in transmitting his design, born of fear and despair, to his
adolescent son. His delight is not so much in fiendishness
as it is in pride. In spite of his emphasis upon man's in-
significance he feels inwardly that he is better than most
men, for he has seen the meaning of life in a clear way. He
is proud to give his son, Quentin, his knowledge, which will,
he feels, help him to live properly according to the authoritarianism he himself has adopted.

The rebellion of Quentin is centered in his thoughts of
incest. I believe that incest symbolizes a desire of the son
to escape from the problems posed by the conflict in the
family to a state of innocence. It signifies a flight from the
father to some childhood paradise. Quentin's remark to
Caddy is especially significant: *"then you will have only
me then only me then the two of us amid the pointing and
the horror beyond the clear flame."* But incest also symbolizes the rebellion of the son against the father. If he can
acknowledge the evil in himself, overstep the limits of morality and commit the deed, he can defeat the father as lawgiver. Yet at the same time he would like to be punished
for his act of rebellion by Presbyterian punishment. In *The
Sound and the Fury* Quentin cannot yield to his desire, but
he tells his father that he has committed incest with Caddy
because of his need to hear his father condemn it as evil.

The father realizes the nature of the lie. He believes, furthermore, that such things occur every day, and that incest
is not evil. Quentin is, therefore, confused because he has
not yielded to his incestuous desires and *actually* proclaimed
his flight and/or his rebellion. But neither has he learned
of the existence of any age-old values by means of his con-
fession. At Harvard he realizes that he cannot return to his
house; he also realizes that he has not learned to stand alone
because of his father's pessimistic insistence upon weakness
in the past. Quentin Compson believes that his only act of
rebellion failed. This failure forces him to suicide with other
paternal words in his mind: "Father said, That's sad too,
people cannot do anything that dreadful they cannot even
remember tomorrow what seems dreadful today."

A similar pattern exists in *As I Lay Dying*, but here it
is the mother, Addie Bundren, who tries to impose her rigid
conduct upon all her children and her husband. In this
novel the mother is equated with the father because she is
the domineering parent. Addie Bundren believes that she
can force her unquestioning family to bury her in Jefferson.
She wants to perpetuate her design, which accepts the certainty of death in opposition to the uncertainty of life. If
her family can take her corpse to Jefferson and undergo
every sort of unnecessary torment in obedience to her desires, she can feel that, even in death, she has triumphed
over the living. It remains for the neighbors of the Bundrens
to sense the utter foolishness of the journey, but they do not
realize that the cause is not Anse but Addie who now lies
in the coffin. Cora Tull thinks it unnatural for the coffin to
be carried for days in the face of fire, flood, and physical
decay. Doctor Peabody resents Anse's insistence upon burial
in Jefferson. Addie's desire is, then, to force the Bundrens
to become so attached to death in its most horrible physical
aspects that they will not be able to forget it. They will
begin to distrust life as they assume death to be much more
meaningful. Addie, like Mr. Compson, gains satisfaction in
exercising power over other people who are unformed; she
seems to echo his words when she thinks: "She [Cora Tull]
prayed for me because she believed I was blind to sin, wanting me to kneel and pray too, because people to whom sin
is just a matter of words, to them salvation is just words too."

Darl is the rebellious son in *As I Lay Dying*. He realizes

that Addie not only has isolated herself from the other Bundrens but also has isolated Jewel from them. He is very conscious of this separation from his brother Jewel, and he realizes that this is the result of Addie's love for her favorite. But he does more—he understands that Jewel is an illegitimate child belonging not to the Bundren family but to Addie and the real father, Preacher Whitfield. Darl stresses in his communication with Vardaman that, in a sense, he has no mother although Jewel does. Addie is only representative of a design which neglects pity for pride, understanding for domination, life for death. It is quite evident that his mind is as complex as Quentin's. He too sees his problem in the family as one involving more than conflict in the household. Darl's quest is for the meaning of parenthood and childhood, of reality. Unlike Faulkner's early presentation of Bayard, the presentations of Quentin and Darl are of sensitive, mentally confused sons who see the ultimate implications of their situations. Like his counterpart in *The Sound and the Fury*, Darl makes one futile attempt to rebel against the insane journey to Jefferson. He sets fire to a barn. This attempt is not only unsuccessful as the impetus to cessation of the journey—it seems to proclaim to the other Bundrens that *he* is insane. In a sense he—like Quentin—is, because his way of thinking is schizoid. He hates the parent but he submits to her as a result of his own lack of power. He wants to stand alone in the world at large but he cannot even stand alone in the household. He is an intellectual in an environment ruled by physical power and decay. Only when we understand the meaning of the son's problems can we appreciate the complete horror of Darl's understanding of his own insanity in his soliloquy.

It is important that both Christmas in *Light in August* and Bon in *Absalom, Absalom!* are mulattoes. By this symbolic presentation Faulkner means to suggest that the persistent thoughts of the son are as indefinite and chaotic as his blood mixture. His actions cannot have certainty of motive (save the frantic need for self-knowledge) and consequent certainty of purpose. He is not sure about any definite status as an individual because he cannot root himself in either the white or the black community. In *Light in August* and *Absalom, Absalom!* the mulatto seems to enjoy the fact that he can torture the women he sleeps with by informing them that he is a Negro. Yet he refuses to become a member of the black community because he realizes that his very acceptance of his own black blood means his damnation as an abstraction in the personal design of men like Sutpen. In a similar way he cannot become a part of the white race because he hates the Southern community, which cannot accept his mixture at face value. Any commitment seems, therefore, to be dangerous for the mulatto. His ambivalent nature is clearly seen by Gavin Stevens, the Faulknerian spokesman, after he has learned of Christmas' flight to Hightower:

And it was the white blood which sent him to the minister, which rising in him for the last and final time, sent him against all reason and all reality, into the embrace of a chimera. . . . Then I believe that the white blood deserted him for a moment. Just a second . . . allowing the black to rise in its final moment and make him turn upon that on which he had postulated his hope of salvation.

Faulkner looks at the conflict between the father and the son in realistic terms in *Absalom, Absalom!* Thomas Sutpen is *actually* the father of Charles Bon. Sutpen—as I have already indicated—is too intent upon his personal design to gain individual recognition through material conformity to notice any other person in the world. He relates all the things which happen to him to his one design; events are considered to be good only if they fit into this self-imposed standard. Toward the end of the novel Quentin Compson's grandfather says that Sutpen in his innocence assumed that virtue and vice could be measured, like ingredients used in cooking. Charles Bon, the Negro son, tries to teach him that he can never completely renounce—to use Hawthorne's phrase—"the chain of human sympathies." He is not as strong, either mentally or physically, as his white father, but he does have a firm belief in his own rights as an individual. He does not want to accept the money he receives from Sutpen because he is unable to believe the fact that his relationship to his father is to be sold in a financial transaction. Bon's rebellion is not one of outright violence. He seems to be too concerned inwardly with his own inferior status to direct his hatred outward against other people in an active way. Should he submit to his father and "[try] to make [himself] into what [he] thinks he wants [him] to be"? Should he rebel on principle because he cannot look at the world with his father's eyes? What Faulkner says in *Absalom, Absalom!* is that as weak as the son may be in relationship to the rigidity of the father, he still has the ability to express his own needs which, he realizes, are in conflict with the principles of the code. One thing is clear. In his own fumbling way the son is trying to gain "that instant of indisputable recognition" which acknowledges the fact of a bond between himself and the father. Bon says: *"He need not even acknowledge me; I will just let him understand just as quickly that he need not do that; that I do not expect that, will not be hurt by that, just as he will let me know that quickly that I am his son."* Sutpen never does in the novel. Faulkner believes that this quest is tragic in the case of Bon. It creates a violent chain reaction which results in the madness of his brother Henry, the death of his sister, and his own destruction.

The conflict between the father and son is stated in symbolic terms in *Light in August*. Instead of an actual progenitor we are concerned here with five people (Hightower and Hines and Grimm and McEachern and Miss Burden) who resemble Thomas Sutpen in their blind devotion to compulsion and their consequent inability to understand the relationship of father and son. Faulkner's meaning is evident. He wants us to realize the horrible fact that more individuals have a personal design now because of the fundamental anxiety of our age. But the nature of this design is not so bold or grand as the nature of Sutpen's. Only moral and psychological uncertainty force these people to find a sense of security in rigidity of behavior. The other implication of this symbolic use of the father-son relationship in the novel is that modern man does not even have the sexual potency necessary for procreation.

Christmas, like Bon, is the wronged son unsure of his identity in the world. He is perhaps more of an outsider because he does not know the name of his real father. The facts about his birth are mysterious—he was found on the steps of an orphanage on Christmas Eve. In *Light in August* Faulkner seems to suggest that the isolated actions of the son can only be more extreme now. He does not have any sense of traditional values—he is not a gentleman like Bon— or any specific image to rebel against. An entire society composed of many personal designs forces the son to declare his integrity as an individual in the midst of hostility. Christmas, therefore, destroys all things within his reach. The only personal design (if it can be called that) which he has is the acute need to find some sort of acceptance from one being who can forget his rigidity of spirit and sense his blood relationship to this violent man. The continual movement of Christmas is important not as obsessive flight but as the search for new directions of love. In the fifth chapter Faulkner uses an image to strengthen our awareness of this: "He could see . . . a printed sentence, fullborn and already dead *God loves me too* like the faded and weathered letters on a last year's billboard God loves me too." Because the range of Christmas' experience is so great, Faulkner is able to suggest that his plight is universal. The remark of Hightower, "Poor man. Poor mankind . . . ," indicates to us that we have to consider the despised man as more than a case history. His quest is representative of the quest for values (especially the one of identification) in these hard times. His crucifixion, that is, can be our crucifixion.

The rebellion of Christmas against Calvinism is violent. In his youth he could accept the "instructions in faith" of McEachern only because of his need to submit to a towering image of authority. He admired the physical strength and spiritual rigidity of the man who adopted him, and he wanted to prove to himself and to his father image that he too was able to achieve manhood. He learned to respect the Sabbath torture he received in the way only a young person can respect orthodoxy. In *Light in August* Faulkner shows us that Christmas, as he grows up, cannot react passively toward the spokesman for Calvinism. His mind is less complex than Bon's, and we have to consider all of his destructive actions to discover his underlying motives. It is probable that the fundamental humanity of Christmas is in conflict with the cold inhumanity of his father's doctrines which he accepted as a youth. The Sabbath incident continues to come into his consciousness. He remembers his debasement before the black-suited farmer and, although his admiration is never completely lost, his resentment against the brutal justice of McEachern becomes overt. His rebellion begins with his characteristic acts of self-assertion (through whoring) before the "actual representative of the wrathful and retributive Throne." McEachern is destroyed by Christmas at the dance hall as he tries to assume his air of self-righteousness. Then the son attempts to extend his hatred outward against those doctrines which were responsible, in part, for his present plight. He goes into the church to curse the Calvinist Lord. This outburst is the culmination of Joe's need to attack the faith which refuses to pity an individual it has helped to shape into Satan.

Faulkner considers the tragedy of Christmas to be complete when he is forced to discontinue his quest. He commits himself to a definite status before the father out of weariness. Christmas accepts his Negro blood at the end of *Light in August* as he puts on the shoes he has just taken from a black man. His actions fix him as an object (without human feeling) to be destroyed. He defines his own position in Southern society by assuming "the gauge definite and ineradicable of the black tide creeping up his legs, moving from his feet upward as death moves." It seems to him that his forthcoming death offers the only certainty he has ever known in his life. This death is viewed as castration by Faulkner. The son is discovered by the father image, Percy Grimm, who punishes him for his sinful attempts at self-expression. The irony of the situation is that the cessation of rebellion does not really bring Christmas closer to the answers to his questions, or to the recognition of the relationship by his father image. It merely means that he chooses his own kind of destruction by submitting to the environment. Faulkner therefore believes that the son cannot discontinue his quest, cannot expect to clearly define his position in the world, as long as he lives. Unlike the father he must continue to be rootless; his ambivalence is all he has. It makes him—to quote Robert Penn Warren—"although he is sometimes spoken of as a villain, . . . a mixture of heroism and pathos."[1]

Obviously Faulkner as creative artist should condemn the abstract design of the father and regard the quest of the son as necessary. We cannot forget, however, that the very fact of his birth in Mississippi offered a code of values, a sense of tradition, to his developing mind. Faulkner is too

[1] Robert Penn Warren, "William Faulkner," in *William Faulkner: Two Decades of Criticism*, ed. Frederick J. Hoffman and Olga Vickery (East Lansing, Mich.: Michigan State College Press, 1951), p. 97.

much a product of his Southern environment to escape from direct conditioning. His situation is akin to that of Joyce in his closeness to his milieu (even in the midst of rebellion). It is well known that Joyce exiled himself from Ireland because he was not able to tolerate completely the religion and the politics of his homeland. He fled to such places as Zurich and Trieste to write about Ireland for the rest of his life. Faulkner does not rebel as manifestly as Joyce did. He still lives in Mississippi despite the fact that he condemns the rigidity of the social and religious organizations of this region. It is clear that he does, at last, side with the rights which the son represents. The ambivalence of his own mind, however, in regard to the father and what he represents is the psychological conflict which is at the heart of the major novels.

Critics have continued to stress the profound sense of personal meaning which *Absalom, Absalom!* must have for its author. In his introduction Harvey Breit states that this novel is an "extreme work, a kind of fiery laboratory of its author's triumphs and travails."[2] The reasons for his belief are clear. Faulkner is concerned here, as I have already indicated, with the design of Thomas Sutpen, one of the founders of his region, and he must present the implications of this design for his people and himself. In the novel he admires the colossal energies Sutpen uses to build his empire. This ability to progress materially has importance for any Southerner, any American, who delights in individualism of expression, for example, Benjamin Franklin. Faulkner realizes the greatness of this man in battle during the War. But Faulkner is aware at the same time of the deep-rooted needs of Sutpen which compel him to continue his pattern, and to disregard the humanity of Bon. Sutpen is so intent upon self-expression that he does not have any idea of the moral code which embraces his son and himself. He can return to his land without any new awareness of his design or the equality of white and black men.

It is, of course, significant that the narrator of *Absalom, Absalom!* is actually Quentin Compson; Quentin cannot forget his tradition in the cold of New England. He realizes his close association with Sutpen and Bon in this passage: *"Maybe nothing ever happens once and is finished. Maybe*

[2] Harvey Breit, Introduction to William Faulkner, *Absalom, Absalom!* (New York: Modern Library, 1951), p. x.

happen is never once but like ripples moving on, spreading. . . ." The misunderstanding between father and son in the past seems to pertain to his own problems in the present. He discusses and tries to unravel the history of his father's design with an outsider, who can see the implications simply with an air of cynicism. Shreve, the Canadian, turns to Quentin and says: "Now I want you to tell me just one thing more. Why do you hate the South?" Quentin feels inwardly (like Faulkner) that as a man who must choose between good and evil he must be either for or against Sutpen and what he represents. All that he can think about the South, the land with the tragic relationship of father and son, is: *"I dont hate it* he thought, panting in the cold air, the iron New England dark; *I dont. I dont! I dont hate it! I dont hate it!"* When we remember that Quentin eventually kills himself in his first year at Harvard (in *The Sound and the Fury*) we realize that his ambivalence cannot be resolved. His suicide is an attempt to escape from the concrete and realistic evaluations necessary for life. Faulkner is different from his narrator because he *is* able to decide that the design of men like Sutpen is wrong. He understands that it is responsible, in part, for the twisted personalities of Charles Bon and Quentin Compson.

Faulkner introduces a new kind of son into his myth in his later novels, which concern the quest for an understanding of the evil and the goodness of the self. He is able to learn about his own motives, the evil of his region, through association with his spiritual guide, a substitute father. His rebellion—as I shall indicate—is neither violent nor confused like that of Christmas, or Bon, or Darl, or Quentin. It comes after the realization of the natural laws of the universe; it is really the demonstration of good will toward all men. The son is not really crucified. He can endure because of his ability to fight with patience and humility and love. But he can do more. He can help to save the South through his Christian standards of behavior which can inspire other men. He is the image of the Savior in Faulkner's myth, but, as R. W. B. Lewis writes,

> This is not to say that he is intended to represent Christ in a second coming, but only that he moves in a world of light—a light still meagre but definite; a new world in which values have been confirmed by being raised to a higher power; . . . a world so

perpetually new that he sometimes seems to be its only living inhabitant.[3]

In "The Bear" the power of Isaac lies in his spirit, which is able to comprehend the inadequacies of personal and social rigidity in religious terms. He believes that the father has committed the sin of pride (he concerns himself only with personal certainty of position) and the sin of murder (he treats others as objects to be manipulated for his own advancement). The design is the *curse* because it is responsible for destruction. It retards human development because it forces the father to adopt that inflexibility which creates an unusual awareness of absolutism; it is responsible for the feeling of doom. Because of his rigidity the father is unable to notice the beauty and goodness of the world. Isaac understands, furthermore, that the father tries to force other people to accept the standards (his own) of rigidity. Force becomes dominant instead of love. This can result only in the continuance of violence. The son is, as we have seen, forced to rebel against the severity which has corrupted his *Weltanschauung* and made him forget his identity.

In "The Bear" Faulkner makes Isaac realize the fact that this treatment of other people in interpersonal relationships resembles the exploitation of nature for financial gain. The pre-War organization was wrong. Sutpen did not have the right to cut off land for his own property and to use the Negro as a tool for cotton picking. The land was never his to possess. It was there long before the first men came to the region to stake claims, to try to become wealthy plantation owners. Isaac believes in the words of the Bible which prove to him that the possession of land and consequent slavery (in the South) were wrong. Isaac believes that the Civil War *did* prove that there cannot be any such system in the South. The black man was not the cause of the War and the havoc of Reconstruction. It was the white plantation owner who was at fault because he committed many mortal sins. Social rigidity, therefore, *was* and *is* the curse on the land.

However, Isaac does more than realize the sins of the father in the Faulknerian myth. He believes that he must atone for them not with violence but with relinquishment.

[3] R. W. B. Lewis, "The Hero in the New World: William Faulkner's 'The Bear,'" *Kenyon Review*, XIII (1951), 649.

Two of his actions are important in this respect. On his twenty-first birthday Isaac refuses to keep the land he has inherited from Carothers McCaslin. He believes that this legacy is representative of the rigidity of the social organization of the South because it assumes that property rights and white skin are means of distinction. Isaac understands that there can only be a perpeutation of the curse if such distinctions exist. He cannot even repudiate the legacy: "It was never mine to repudiate. It was never Father's and Uncle Buddy's to bequeath to me to repudiate, because it was never Grandfather's to bequeath them to bequeath to me to repudiate." Isaac believes that the land still belongs only to the Lord. In a related way Faulkner tries to demonstrate the fact that Isaac sees the evil of personal design. Isaac's own grandfather had refused—like Sutpen—to acknowledge the Negro children he had spawned. There was not any active effort on his part to help them because of the "accident of their own paternity." The only acknowledgment of his blood relationship to these Negro children was in the will he left to his descendants. Isaac tries to reimburse the children of Carothers McCaslin, his Negro relatives, with a symbolic "Legacy, a Thing possessing weight to the hand and bulk to the eye and even audible: a silver cup filled with gold pieces and wrapped in burlap and sealed with his godfather's ring in hot wax." He believes that the donation of this heirloom can show them his ability to acknowledge the rights of other beings. He recognizes his moral responsibility in a way that Hightower cannot because he lacks one inflexible standard of behavior. His spirit is strong enough to accept the fact that he is not different—he and all men are brothers. In "The Bear" Isaac is at one with the actual workings of the universe. He is certain of the meaning of his Christian potentialities for atonement and charity, and he becomes not a landowner but a carpenter because "if the Nazarene had found carpentering good for the life and ends He had assumed and elected to serve, it would be all right too for Isaac McCaslin."

This is the final lesson which he learns from Sam Fathers. It is significant that his teacher is part Negro and part Indian, for he is able to relate himself to both races. Sam does not have an exaggerated vision of his ancestors, although they are older and more enduring than the Confederate generals.

He is able to understand that Old Ben, as a symbol of the wildness of nature which must be tamed, is more important than this heritage. The Bear has "furious immortality" for him. His recognition of the fact makes him as fertile in his old age as the natural scene which is his home. He is not childless in the story because of any impotence; the whole meaning of "The Bear" lies in the fact that he can regard Isaac McCaslin (though he is related to the father who destroyed his own people) as his son and that this son can appreciate the values of Sam Fathers and adopt them as his own. Their communion is an indication of their ability to understand natural laws. Their powerful spirits enable them to see each other as hunters without the need for "instrumentalized" designs.

Like Isaac, Charles Mallison Jr. in *Intruder in the Dust* learns to become a man through his involvement with the substitute father. Even before the actual day he realizes that the Negro, Lucas Beauchamp, is involved in murder, he has already experienced some sort of ritualistic initiation. It was not one of hunt but of baptism. Four years ago when he was twelve Charles fell into an ice pond, and was unable to get out of the chilled waters without the aid of Lucas' directions and bodily assistance. This communication is the genesis of the boy's learning experiences in the novel. When he discovers in the present that this Negro—who acted in a compassionate way which seemed to be foreign to *all* black men—has been found near the corpse of a white man, he thinks inwardly that he cannot be involved with him again, because Lucas does not fit the region's definition. He does not understand what Lucas desires from him of all people. The confusion of his mind is increased when he is told, commanded in a sense, to unearth the white man's grave in spite of the fact that the territory around it is possibly surrounded by white supremists. This task is akin to Isaac's symbolic outings and, like Isaac, Charles is afraid at first. But he submits to this guide in order to return as a man with necessary knowledge of his responsibilities in his family, his native region, and the outside world. The boy discovers that Lucas, whom he would have liked to think of as guilty before, is, in reality, innocent and understands more about race relations than the white supremists do. Charles is able to realize the unusual capacities of men like Lucas who have come to terms with their own natures and the failure of the social system. He knows that the Negro can also endure because he has always experienced the hardships of life, hardships *he* has never known. The Negro has fought for so many years in the face of conflict that he has been able to recognize further potentialities for compassion and love and hope. He— like the hunter and the man who uncovers graves in the face of possible death—does not need false security. He has his own spirit, which is secure because it has emerged victorious through conflict with all oppressors. By being an intruder in the dust, by observing his own tendency toward evil, Charles Mallison Jr. realizes that he has become a man even though he cannot yet completely express this in words. When he consciously expresses this knowledge he can, like Isaac, become a savior.

The new son appears, of course, in A *Fable*. The Corporal, like his two predecessors, is able to discover the inadequacies of his father's authoritarian demands not through warlike rebellion but through ritualistic initiation in a peaceful yet strong way. It is clear that war is an agent in the novel in the same way the bear hunt is. But here the action encompassed is of an expansive nature covering the entire world. Like Isaac, the Corporal has an opportunity to kill for selfish ends, to conform to the rigidity of his environment (military, as opposed to Southern society in Isaac's case). He refuses because of the understanding that if he too kills men, this will not prove that he has strength—it will only demonstrate his inability to survive without assistance. The Corporal is concerned with the training for himself and for all men to assert self-sufficiency in the face of authority. This is the reason he leads the mutiny to end the world war. The rules of natural law involved are more important to him than the martial rules of his father, the General, who decrees the absolute necessity of war.

In the temptation scene between the Corporal and the General we see that an understanding has finally been reached between the father and the son in the Faulknerian myth. Here the son and the father actually communicate in more than a purely verbal sense. Both of them realize the nature of each other's personalities and philosophies. The General admires the courage of his son, and he sympathizes with his desire to help people. But he feels that most people need the strength of authority to direct their actions. Like Mr. Compson, the General sees the folly and weakness of men, their motivation for wanting to be led. Thus he firmly believes that he is actually helping humanity, and he refuses to accept his son's philosophy. The Corporal, on the other hand, acknowledges that he is the son of the General because he can see his own tendencies toward absolutism. He is able to understand that—in the words of Reverend Tobe Sutter-field—

Evil is a part of man, evil and sin and cowardice, the same as repentance and being brave. You got to believe in all of them or believe in none of them. Believe that man is capable of all of them, or he aint capable of none.

This comprehension, then, of his own capacities for good and evil helps him to see that he could have become like his father, if he had not conquered his own inclinations. The Corporal knows this: if he submits to his father who cannot break away from his design of continuance of war, he is voluntarily accepting the temptation of assuming the other role than that of savior—the destroyer. His own coming to terms with the meaning of evil in himself and the external war enables him to be brave in his martyrdom at the hands of his father. The Corporal hopes with humility—as do Isaac in "The Bear" and Charles in *Intruder in the Dust*—that other men will look at his example and see the necessity of combating absolutism in order to gain freedom. This is the ultimate reason for his refusal of the temptations.

Remembering the intellectual turmoil of the early sons, Quentin and Darl, and the physical violence of Christmas and Bon, and understanding the spiritual potentialities of the later sons, Isaac and Charles Mallison Jr., we can appreciate the simplicity of the Corporal's statement at the end of this scene because we can see how much the sons (and the fathers) have developed in the myth. The scene and the myth of Faulkner end with these lines:

'Good-bye Father,' the corporal answered him.
'Not good-bye,' the old general said. 'I am durable too . . . Remember whose blood it is that you defy me with.'

THE WOMEN

3

THE WOMEN

Faulkner's women are, for the most part, stereotypes who live in a world of their own. One feels that they are elusive because Faulkner cannot adequately describe their feelings or see them as well-rounded individuals. I will try to indicate that his women fall into two large groupings: the sexual and the asexual. This crude division is characteristic of many of our writers—Cooper, Melville, Mark Twain—who characterize men well but fail to create meaningful portraits of women. In part this failure is related to their concern with law, business relationships, hunting, but it also indicates that they, like so many American men who think of Woman as either Marilyn Monroe or Eleanor Roosevelt, suffer from our cultural attitude toward "the second sex."

In his first novel, *Soldiers' Pay*, Faulkner writes about Cecily Saunders, a Fitzgerald heroine. She is quite inviting to almost all of the men in her Georgia town as she walks along the street, or pulls up her stockings, or brushes against table legs, and Faulkner also delights in such things. Cecily is conscious of her sexual attractiveness, and this attractiveness not only consumes many of her waking hours but enables her to get whatever she wants. There is a quality of willfulness, of the need for continual self-assertion, about her. She toys with Jones, the fat satyr; with George Farr, the innocent, lustful boy; even with her father (in a less obvious way); she refuses to marry poor Donald Mahon, the dying veteran, after she realizes that she can't love him physically, giving little thought to the consequences of her refusal. Faulkner seems to be more aware of her fanatic will, as *Soldiers' Pay* progresses, than of her beauty. We begin to fear and to despise Cecily's power over men. In an outburst of hysteria, she says at one point, "I am sick and tired of men." Faulkner's condemnation of her grasping narcissism is introduced artificially, as it is throughout the novel, when she lies on her bed, thinking of marriage:

> The door closed behind him [her father] and she lay staring at its inscrutable, painted surface, running her fingers lightly over her breasts, across her belly, drawing concentric circles upon her body beneath the covers, wondering how it would feel to have a baby, hating that inevitable time when she'd have to have one, blurring her slim epicenity, blurring her body with pain . . .

Cecily refuses, through fantasy, to bear children because of the possible consequences to her body. Later she does marry George Farr, who can offer sexual satisfaction. Faulkner does not describe Cecily's marriage (he is never to describe normal marriage in his work), but he gives us a fleeting vision of her subsequent unhappiness when she returns to the town with her husband:

> It was Mr. and Mrs. George Farr: they saw Cecily's stricken face as she melted graceful and fragile and weeping into her father's arms. And here was Mr. George Farr morose and thunderous behind her. Ignored.

It seems as if their marriage has been a sexual conflict to dominate or to be dominated; Cecily has probably been victorious.

In many ways the characterization of the two flappers in *Mosquitoes*, Patricia and Jenny, is similar to the one of Cecily. Both Patricia and Jenny are physically appealing in the 1920's sense, "with the uncomplex awkwardness of calves or colts, with the two little knobs for breasts and indicated buttocks that, except for their soft look, might well belong to a boy of fifteen." The girls disturb the men aboard Mrs. Maurier's boat by their mixture of sex and innocence, of tomboyishness and sophistication. However, the emphasis upon their willfulness is, again, the most significant element. Patricia refuses to be passive; she talks back to her aunt (who deserves .it), condemns the "artists," and persuades the steward, David, to flee from the boat to a near-by island. This elopement is a curious incident. Faulkner tries desperately to show us the needless, willy-nilly inclinations of Patricia, and how they can be destructive to the passive man. David does not *really* want to leave the boat. He is unhappy, frightened, as he and Patricia have their "grand" adventure, and his face shows it. But she does not care—that is, not until both of them begin to be stifled by the heat and become thirsty. Then she, like Cecily, becomes hysterical because circumstances are in conflict with her selfish desires:

"I must go on," she repeated. "Make me go on, David. I don't want to die here. Make me go on, I tell you." Her face was flushed: he could see blood pumping in her throat, and holding her he knew sharp and utter terror. "What must I do?" she was saying. "You ought to know. Don't you know what to do? I'm sick, I tell you."

After she has to admit her foolishness to David, who has carried her most of the way, they return to Mrs. Maurier's *Nausikaa*. The consequences are more painful for the steward than for his companion. He quits his job because has has been disappointed by his relationship with Patricia, and he cannot stay with her any longer aboard the boat. But she continues to be adolescent, wanting to see "mountains," as long as she can tower above them. Faulkner believes that she has learned nothing. In a way, he has learned no more about female psychology; he has merely repeated his superficial, "romantic" description of the flapper.

Like her predecessors, Temple Drake in *Sanctuary* is, at first, a flapper intent upon enjoyment, but she becomes utterly corrupt. Faulkner believes that her vanity and will to power expose her to the malicious advances of a man who cannot be swayed—Popeye. In the rape scene she is powerless because circumstances oppose and terrify her (actually Popeye is suffering from the same inadequacies), her potentialities to fight evil have never been tested before. But Temple wants the opportunity to fall so that she can become completely immoral. She wants to attack her father's conservatism ("My father's a judge"), to live in a brothel, to sleep with any man who is attractive. She *does* fall as a result of her own need to carry her vanity as far as it can go. In a cultural sense she symbolizes the American girl who wants to go to Hollywood. I think this accounts for Faulkner's spleen. He despises Temple because she has been swayed by *glamour*. She accepts evil as an attractive and exciting force, and it carries the same connotative value for her as the sex appeal she has heard about at street corners or in parked cars. Temple is actually so weak-willed that she has been raped symbolically long before her encounter with Popeye. This later meeting merely reinforces the qualities she already possesses and makes them more bearable, because she can now blame the criminal elements in our culture for her downfall.

It is misleading to accuse Temple of being stereotyped. She is a complex person who is unsure of growing up, who desires and fears men (especially after she is attacked), a creature of the modernism which equates sex with evil. Faulkner's anger is extreme. He hates Temple—perhaps unjustly, some will say—knowing well that she and her youthful counterparts *like* what they are doing but don't want to admit it. Her testimony helps to convict an honest man, Goodwin, of Popeye's crime and, ironically, makes the community, including her father, think of her as a "ruined, defenseless child."

In the short story "Elly" the heroine is almost the sister of Temple. She is also sexually frantic, lying in the veranda of her family's house with any man whose appearance is "decent." But unlike Temple she does not have any actual loss of virginity (she says "No. Not now . . ." to the men) to use as an excuse for her later actions. She is forthright with her deaf grandmother who sees her at play but does not hear her cruel words of denunciation. Elly rebels against the conservatism of her family in her affair with Paul de Montigny, who is part black. She believes that she can run away from the ugly town by marrying him; unfortunately he wants only to sleep with her. During a wild automobile ride, Elly, sitting between Paul and her grandmother, grabs the wheel in an attempt to kill the old woman. Paul resists but cannot stop her. The car goes over the edge of a precipice.

This scene is another vivid demonstration of Faulkner's attitude toward the willful flapper. The evil of an Elly, whose maladjustment was produced by her social environment, replaces the undeveloped corruption of a Patricia or a Cecily. It is clear that he cannot tolerate the needless destruction which narcissism and the desire for escape can bring both to the woman and to the people involved with her. But is Faulkner's characterization of the flapper limited? I think he does not suggest adequately the abuses which are responsible, in part, for a Temple or an Elly. He is content merely to call these women corrupt without any complete investigation of male influences—in short, the final impression is that his limited investigation is, except perhaps for Temple, unfair and sensational.

The other women in Faulkner's work who fall into this large grouping, the sexual, are negatively associated with sex—that is, they have tried to repress their libido (in the Freudian sense), but it asserts itself in devious and corrupt ways. They are perhaps more abnormal than the flapper, for they have adopted the rigidity of the male and have lived with it for a long time. Faulkner is able to characterize these masculine women more adequately than Cecily, Patricia, or Elly.

In *Light in August* Miss Burden is known throughout the community as a lover of Negroes. Her masculine sense of purpose enables her to take care of the weekly correspondence she receives from the young students at Negro schools scattered across the South. Her moral responsibility seems to be evident when she travels to these schools to help in the solution of various problems which pertain to the education and health of the Negro race. But Faulkner believes that her efforts cannot be constructive or valid because Miss Burden is a creature without the ability to understand the motives which force her to act the way she does. Her motivation is, to a large degree, a result of past indoctrination. When she was four years old her father took her to the graves of her ancestors. She did not want to go. "I don't know why I didn't want to . . . I think it was something about father, something that came from the cedar grove to me, through him. . . . I would never be able to forget it." On that day Miss Burden learned that some members of her family were killed after a dispute over Negro voting rights during the Reconstruction period. But they did not really accept the fact that the black man had the rights of the white man (although they seemed to think so). They emphasized the fact that the Negro race was "doomed and cursed to be forever and ever a part of the white race's doom and curse for its sins. . . . The curse of every white child that ever was born and ever will be born." Miss Burden accepted the doctrines of her father because of her own childhood inadequacies before his towering image of strength and "wisdom."

It is, of course, significant that Miss Burden has a love

affair with Christmas. Faulkner is trying to stress the nature
of her sexual ambivalence in the relationship because he believes that she is too concerned with the personal design of
her ancestors to care about her natural function as a woman.
Even Joe realizes that she is a "dual personality: the one the
woman . . . , a horizon of physical security and adultery
if not pleasure; the other the mantrained muscles and the
mantrained habit of thinking born of heritage and environment." Miss Burden is both a puritan and a nymphomaniac;
she is in a state of continual conflict. The violence of her
passion is a release of the drive which her design has in-
hibited or restrained in the past. Miss Burden expresses herself in sexual intercourse, but her means of expression are
only corrupt and perverse. Christmas feels that "[it] was as
though he had fallen into a sewer." The relationship ends
tragically. Miss Burden reaches the menopause and her loss
of fertility is associated in her mind at first with pregnancy.
But the realization that she cannot bear any children, that
she cannot be a mother, is the motive which compels her at
last to yield completely to the personal design which she has
never really abandoned. She seems to assume the image of
the father for Joe Christmas when she decides that he as a
Negro (as a symbol of the curse upon herself and her region)
fits into her compulsive pattern. Her attempt to save his soul
is similar to the attempts of McEachern to save Joe's soul
on the Sabbath when he tried to teach him the catechism.
Christmas can only rebel against her rigid sense of purpose
which disregards his individual needs. He therefore destroys the "sexless" Miss Burden because he now thinks of
her as McEachern.

Drusilla in *The Unvanquished* is also attached to the Civil
War. She believes wholeheartedly in the Confederate cause,
not considering its fundamental inhumanity, and she discovers that she must act like a man to defend it. Drusilla
adopts masculine attire, speech, and means of action; she
engages in active combat along with her husband-to-be,
John Sartoris, against the invading Union forces. After Sartoris attacks the carpetbaggers and, in turn, disenfranchises
the Negroes, their marriage takes place. Drusilla's submission to the code of the old order produces extreme consequences. It is difficult to believe that she has a marriage in
which she and her husband are equals; she worships his

glamorous will and she accepts things as a child would. In "An Odor of Verbena," the most important story in the collection, she tries to assume an authoritarian role similar to that of John Sartoris when she commands her stepson, Bayard, to avenge his father's murder. She does this in a curious way, a way which is both harsh and passionate: she offers him two dueling pistols and a kiss. But Bayard refuses. He does not kill Redmond, his father's murderer, because of his belief in the inadequacies of his father's dream and, upon returning to the house, he is told that his sobbing stepmother has left by train, her desires having been thwarted. Like Joanna and Cecily, Drusilla has reverted to hysteria in the face of the possible defeat of her will.

In what is perhaps his most famous story, "A Rose for Emily," Faulkner characterizes another woman whose repression of her sexual needs leads to perversion. Miss Emily Grierson, a member of one of the oldest families in Jefferson, lives alone in her frame house, afraid to go out after her father dies and her sweetheart deserts her. Emily's attachment to the will of the father—it is said that he had driven all the young men away—has stunted her growth. She keeps a fading crayon portrait of him, tries to deny the fact that he has been dead for three days (the townspeople bury him by force), and wants to assume his role as father when she informs the group of people who come to collect taxes that they should see Sartoris. In her own way Miss Emily is as masculine as Joanna or Drusilla, but like the two women, she discovers that she cannot contain her feelings, that she has to express herself through a sexual relationship. Homer Baron represents wild virility, and she has an affair with him. Of course this cannot last. Her passionate, almost sexual relationship with her dead father forces her to distrust the living body of Homer and to kill him so that he will resemble the dead father she can never forget. But after her own death, the townspeople enter the house and find to their horror that she has slept next to Homer's corpse all these years. It is, of course, ironic fate that Miss Emily's body joins

the representatives of those august names where they lay in the cedar-bemused cemetery among the ranked and anonymous graves of Union and Confederate soldiers who fell at the battle of Jefferson.

Faulkner's disgust with women who tighten their feelings so much that they become men enables him to give a wonderful analysis of Miss Emily Grierson's necrophilia. He distrusts her rigid adherence to the male world because it not only perverts the woman's desire for natural affection and motherhood—it creates social tensions. This is quite clear in another story, "Dry September." Minnie Cooper discovers, after an unfortunate relationship with the alcoholic cashier in the bank, that men are not to be trusted—they want only sex, not spiritual companionship. She learns to deprive herself of any desires she may have to find another, better man, and she follows the same pattern into rigidity—symbolically, Emily's love of death—as necessary retreat. Unfortunately Minnie Cooper imagines, as a sex wish-fulfillment, that she has been raped by a Negro. The community accepts her fantasy as real, and it decides to take care of him, even though some people realize that she is a bit mad. Of course Minnie, like Joanna and Emily, is stereotyped—the old maid looking under her bed at night. But Faulkner is able to suggest the frightening consequences when twisted female psychology is turned against innocence and destroys it. Completely willful and unthinking, the repressed woman is more violent than a Cecily—and more malevolent. The downfall of these repressed women is expressed in vicious ways, but it is associated with the spiritual degradation of the New Woman, trying to live in the business world of men, forgetting about the family, "the fire and the hearth." Faulkner succeeds in his attempt to shock us into this understanding as Ibsen does in *Hedda Gabler*.

Now we come to the other grouping of Faulkner's women: the asexual. Here we can find traditional images of the mother and the grandmother (or old spinster), both of whom have lost their active association with *Eros*. It is obvious that Faulkner, has respect for these women, knowing they cannot use their beauty or repression to destroy men. This is not to say that they don't exhibit strong will power. All of his women do, but, as I will try to indicate, in the case of a Lena or Miss Habersham, the will, although aggressive, is humanitarian. And there is a quality of affection which conflicts with Faulkner's horror, or fear, or plain disgust, toward the women I have already mentioned.

Aunt Jenny Du Pre is one of Faulkner's sweet-sour old

women. In *Sartoris* her presence seems to dominate the
household (except perhaps for the dead general) as she
commands the Negro servant to keep busy, narrates stories,
and tells Old Bayard to have his mole looked at. Aunt Jenny
has a sharp tongue, but she also has an inner quality which
is evident in the garden scenes. (These scenes are symbolic,
although crudely handled, of her association with nature, of
her "down-to-earth" consciousness. They demonstrate, although less forcibly than her conversation, that she has not
given herself to the new culture invading Jefferson.) Her
ire is curiously aroused when she considers the foolishness
of the Sartoris clan, especially the reckless grandson, Bayard.
She may spin yarns of ante-bellum bravery, of the glorious
strength of John Sartoris, but she senses, without completely
admitting it to herself, that the family is doomed. After
Bayard, whom she would have whipped for his wild driving,
dies in the plane crash, she *does* admit these feelings to his
wife, Narcissa, as they talk about their newborn son. This
Cassandra-like strain is important; it indicates both her
shrewdness and strict moral standard. In the story, "There
Was a Queen," which describes her last days, Faulkner contrasts Aunt Jenny's strength to the weakness of Narcissa, who
sacrifices her honor by sleeping with a blackmailer in order
to retrieve her stolen letters. The old woman is shocked to
hear the news. In a final scene she puts her hat firmly upon
her head and sits erect, near the window. She dies the same
evening. Faulkner's high regard for this severe woman is
apparent in his last description of her:

. . . beside the dead window the old woman sat motionless, indicated only by that single faint gleam of white hair, as though
for ninety years life had died slowly up her spare, erect frame,
to linger for a twilit instant about her head before going out,
though life itself had ceased.

Although Rosa Coldfield in *Absalom, Absalom!* is suffering from neurotic attachments which have distorted her, in
a way she is like Aunt Jenny. Perhaps she is a more complex
person, because Faulkner tries to show us both her early and
later years; we know *more* about the reasons for her grim
determination. During adolescence Rosa's extreme isolation
from her father—who, in Shreve's words, "nailed himself up
in the attic to keep from being drafted into the Rebel army

and starved to death"—made her into a crotchety, violent, and perceptive old maid. She is obsessed by Sutpen (she calls him "the demon") largely as a result of her own psychological inadequacies, her fearful need for a strong-man type. But Faulkner gives Rosa Coldfield an awareness, in the midst of many unreasoned denunciations, of the possible meaning of Thomas Sutpen. She senses that he *is* a destroyer of the family, the old order, in spite of his heroic attempts to reconstruct and perpetuate his design after the War has been lost. The strength of her will is shown at the end of the novel when she drags Quentin Compson with her to the mansion in order to make him understand its total meaning for her and for the citizens of the new South, before the death which she expects. Her preoccupation with the male conflicts of rigidity and rebellion has, it is true, stifled her only need for affection, but it has also enabled her to escape from the abuse of Mr. Compson, who says of women: "They lead beautiful lives . . . lives not only divorced from, but irrevocably excommunicated from, all reality." Rosa Coldfield emerges as a sick, implacable person—it is hard to say woman—probing the nature of the historical process, assuming the responsibilities of Southern men, "in the face of pain and annihilation which would make the most spartan man resemble a puling boy." Faulkner may look with uneasiness at her spinsterhood, but he can only admire her desire for truth and justice.

Rosa Millard in *The Unvanquished* is simpler than her namesake, because Faulkner seems to be intent upon romanticizing his people and incidents here. (Most of the stories were written for *The Saturday Evening Post*.) It is difficult for us to accept her theatrical actions—of hiding the two boys under her skirt when she is questioned about them or stealing mules from the Union forces. However, she exhibits the same kind of aggressive benevolence as the other two women. Rosa Millard tries to rebuild her neighbors' farms, to keep the Confederate spirit high in the face of oncoming defeat, by distributing the mules to the community. She keeps what she calls her "accounts" in a ledger, carefully taking stock of the progress the owners are making. These business transactions occur in the church. Rosa is, like the other two old women, a religious person who realizes the nature of her sins and tries to confess them to a Calvinist Lord. The sins in this case range from plain cussing, to wounding Northerners, to stealing. But Faulkner never goes into her conflict between religion and economics, actually one of the significant conflicts of American society. Rosa Millard's prayers have a fairy-tale quality. Acute moral understanding seems to be less important than conventional ritual to her. Of all Faulkner's characterizations of old Southern women, Rosa seems the most romantic. Unaware of her region's inadequacies or, for that matter, of her own psychological problems, triumphant even in death, Rosa Millard is more conventional than individual, more unreal than real; she is Mark Twain's widow Douglas seen in a rose-colored haze.

The "kinless" spinster, Miss Habersham, is also romantically characterized in *Intruder in the Dust*, but she does emerge as a person, motivated by the need to see justice prevail in the contemporary South. She cannot believe that Lucas Beauchamp, the Negro, killed a white man; she knows inwardly that he and his wife, Molly (born the same week as she, seventy years ago) are good people, in spite of what some white supremists condemn as *black* skin. Miss Habersham is a woman of action, and, like Rosa Coldfield, she takes on a man's role when men are too busy or too malicious to cope with a great moral problem. She decides to risk her life by driving to the graveyard in the evening with the two boys, Aleck Sander and Charles Mallison Jr., to uncover the grave and discover the identity of the corpse. After their dark adventure, Charles knows for truth—although he had half-heard it in the past from old Ephraim, a slave—that

> If you got something outside the common run thats got to be done and cant wait, dont waste your time on the menfolks; they works on . . . the rules and cases. Get the womens and children at it; they works on the circumstances.

But Miss Habersham, not content to do only this to help the Negroes she loves, asks to keep guard in the prison to prevent any possible lynching. In this description, Faulkner suggests that she can be an inspirational force to those citizens who refuse to do anything about the current situation and merely retreat into personal problems. Although Miss Habersham frequently acts as if she were in an adventure story, she receives more admiration for her good sense than most of the other women I have mentioned and, indeed, most of the men. Faulkner is able to make her both a living reality (as she tries to get through traffic in her truck and loses her way) and a symbol of what he praises in Man: the potentialities to respect and save himself without the artificiality of ritual. And she is reflected in Faulkner's image of the mother.

In his first novel, *Soldiers' Pay*, Faulkner introduces a woman who is to appear in almost all of his works: the mother. Emmy, however, is only a mother symbolically; she does not actually give birth to a child. Her sole function in the novel is to demonstrate, by contrast to Cecily, the qualities of self-sacrifice and devotion to a cause. Emmy loves Donald, the wounded and dying veteran, as a mother would her child, taking care of him in spite of the fact that he is not conscious of her assistance. It had not always been like this. In the past their adolescent love was mainly sexual, and it slowly assumed spiritual or moral significance, when Donald left for the war and Emmy moved into his home, after being called a whore by her own father. She lives daily with the one concern of caring for her unacknowledged lover. I think that Faulkner stresses the spontaneity of her actions, the nonreflective emotions which assert themselves, as she looks at Donald, and remembers the day she lost her virginity. It is striking that her memories are filled with pictures of the woods and the moon. These associations are to suggest to us that she is related to the physical setting, and that her love is born of nature. Emmy, unfortunately, does not marry the veteran because he is, at first, engaged to Cecily, who is more beautiful than she. But she does not care too much. She goes proudly about her work, nursing him, hoping desperately that he will improve and love her again. He never does. When Cecily leaves him to elope with George Farr, Mrs. Powers (another good woman) marries him because she does *say* that she can love him, that he needs her love. Donald Mahon dies a few months later, and, on the day of his burial, Emmy is seduced by the corrupt Januarius Jones. (The seduction is symbolic of the betrayal of spirit by sex, of nature by materialism. It will appear again in *Sanctuary* and *The Wild Palms*.) The reader is shocked at this concluding incident because Faulkner has succeeded in portraying a pure woman throughout the novel—a woman whose simple thoughts and actions are these:

Marry him? Yes! Yes! Let him be sick: she would cure him; let him be a Donald that had forgotten her—she had not forgotten: she could remember enough for both of them. Yes! Yes! she cried, soundlessly, stacking dishes, waiting for Mrs. Powers to ask her [if she wants to marry Donald after Cecily has run away] again. Her red hands were blind, tears splashed fatly on her wrists. Yes! Yes! trying to think it so loudly that the other must hear her. . . . But the other woman only stood in the door watching her busy back. So she gathered up the dishes slowly, there being no reason to linger any longer. Keeping her head averted she carried the dishes to the pantry poor, slowly, waiting for the other to speak again. But the other woman said nothing and Emmy left the room, her pride forbidding her to let the other see her tears.

The woman as earth mother has an important place in Faulkner's myth of rigidity because she is separated from the conflict between the father and the son. She does not seem to exist in the male world which is disturbed by the need for the rigidity of personal design or by the rebellion against rigidity. It is clear that her intellect is less complex than that of the male. But Faulkner demonstrates the fact that she is close to the world of nature; her "nature" is like the flow of the moon and the seasons. She has cyclical movement represented by the act of menstruation which is not only a ceremony of periodic filth, as Joe Christmas believes it to be, but an indication of her closeness to the actual workings of the universe. Even Miss Burden, who is not a complete woman, can feel that her menopause is "something out of the darkness, the earth, the dying summer itself." The actions of the woman are therefore seen as spontaneous and reflexive by Faulkner, and they are not motivated by the abstract notions which perplex the daily routines of men. It is clear that she should recognize her function as the progenitor of children. She does not have to assert her individuality in any calculated or violent way, Faulkner believes, because the very acceptance of her femininity implies an acceptance of the orderly nature of the universe and her place in it. He believes, furthermore, that this kind of psychological and spiritual commitment to her status as woman is necessary before she can become "the Passive and Anonymous whom God had created to be not alone the recipient and receptacle of the seed of His body but His spirit too, which is truth."

Lena Grove—almost the Faulknerian "archetype" of the earth mother—is first viewed in *Light in August* as she walks along the road during her pregnancy. We learn of her important connection with nature from this picture. She is close to the green fields (perhaps to the grove which is symbolized by her name), and she is trying to find the male progenitor, Lucas Burch, and marry him so that her child can have a "real" father. It is clear that she is modest and faithful in her actions. But Faulkner also wants to show us that she has more than individual goodness—she is responsible for the goodness of other people (like the Armstids and then Byron Bunch) who try to help her reach her destination. There is something marvelous about her physical condition which is indicative of the too easily forgotten fecundity of nature. I believe that the state of motherhood is symbolic throughout the novel. We can remember the kindness of McEachern's wife on the Sabbath after her husband has brutally mistreated Joe. She seems to want spontaneously to help Joe (by giving him food) but her offer of assistance is rejected. He prefers the punishment of the father, which is more predictable and, therefore, more meaningful to him than the reflexive actions of this woman. In a related way Mrs. Hines offers to help deliver Lena's child, although she is painfully trying to discover the circumstances of Joe's birth from her deranged husband. This woman's illusion that the child is her daughter Milly's little boy emphasizes the fact that all women seem to be bound affectionately by the timeless act of birth, and their tie is not destroyed by any vision they may have of the conflict of present conditions.

The mythic association of woman and nature is hinted at in *Sanctuary*. Horace Benbow, the aristocrat who tries to fight evil and is defeated, thinks at one point: "That's why we know nature is a she; because of that conspiracy between female flesh and female season. So each spring I could watch the reaffirmation of the old ferment. . . . That's why nature is 'she' and Progress is 'he': nature made the grape arbor, but Progress invented the mirror." Only when we realize that the complete female acceptance of this association is meaningful can we realize the significance of a seemingly incoherent passage in the same novel. Popeye, the man with the pattern of destruction, in *Requiem for a Nun*, is about to rape Temple with a corncob. His action not only defeminizes her—as I have already indicated—but forces her to adopt a conscious design in her later life and prevents her from being a conscientious parent. The vision which she has of her own loss of femininity points the way toward this later "unnaturalness." It is, in a sense, her baptism.

The contrast between the woman who accepts her role as mother and the woman who fights this role is shown in *The Wild Palms*. Charlotte believes that romantic love is wonderful, that she can live with it illegitimately, away from the encroachments of civilization. But she and Harry discover that this love cannot exist in a vacuum, and in the mining camp, in Chicago, and in the summer house near the palms, they learn painfully that it can be influenced by economics, group ostracism, and the threat of an unwanted pregnancy. So Charlotte must fight the pregnancy because it will destroy her unthinking desire "to take the illicit love and make it respectable." What Faulkner suggests is that, ironically, this attempt compels her to adopt an unnatural role as a destroyer not only of marriage and family, but of her own life. Her abortion, which her lover bungles after having performed a successful one on a married friend, is responsible for her subsequent illness and death. In "The Old Man" sections of the novel, we meet a woman who accepts her pregnancy like Lena Grove. This woman is, of course, opposed to romantic love because she is faithful to one of the natural laws of the universe—childbirth—and she is able to communicate her belief emotionally to the Mississippi jailbird, at least for the length of the river journey, that responsibility is more important than escape. He battles the flood with her so that she can have her child and keep it alive until they reach land. He becomes, through her assistance, a married man, in a sense, rather than a bachelor. This pregnant woman (cosmically unnamed) is seen as part of nature—this time the natural element is water (lovers like Charlotte and Harry too frequently forget this role of nature at the expense of those who are to be born). She and the convict endure—the others perish.

Two other women should be mentioned. Dewey Dell—notice her name!—in *As I Lay Dying* is similar, at first glance, to Lena in the embodiment of fecundity. When she sits down, Faulkner writes, "her wet dress shapes . . . those mammalian ludicrosities which are the horizons and the valleys of the earth." Eula in *The Hamlet* also seems to serve the identical function. She is "a moist blast of spring's liquorish corruption, a pagan triumphal prostration before the supreme uterus." But these two women are involved in iniquity of sorts, and they are not successful in marital relationships. Dewey Dell is unable to marry the man who fathered her child. She does not want to bear his child; she goes with her family, not really to take her mother's corpse to the cemetery, but to purchase abortive "pills" in the town's drugstore. Eula wants to marry Flem Snopes, the parasitic man of commerce invading the South, in spite of his impotence and her pregnancy.

I believe, in conclusion, that Faulkner's women are rather superficial; they remain fanciful creations of a man who cannot grant them emotional completeness but limits them to extreme, willful, and isolated desires. Consequently his fiction suffers in part from his inability to portray women as both physical and spiritual. Furthermore I believe that Faulkner does not give his full attention to the many-sided problems of women because he is more interested in the conflict between father and son, design and quest for identity. He inspects man's world and the women who try to enter it, equating "feminine" women (those he knows least about) with nature. The result is types rather than complex individuals.

THE TECHNIQUE OF OPPOSITIONS

4

THE TECHNIQUE OF OPPOSITIONS

In his review of *The Portable Faulkner* Robert Penn Warren asks, "To what extent does Faulkner work in terms of polarities . . . ? How much does he employ a line of concealed (or open) dialectic progression as a principle for his fiction?"[1]

The technique of oppositions is apparent in *As I Lay Dying*. Faulkner uses Addie's design, which exists even after she dies, as the controlling symbol. Her children as well as her husband react to the rigidity which she knows is "something in [their] secret and selfish [lives]," although they are, for the most part, unaware of it. But Faulkner also uses the journey to Jefferson as the main plot line. By this I mean that the Bundrens are involved with the external environment as well as with their internal compulsions. The technique of oppositions is broadly this: the conflict between design and events of the journey, between rigidity and movement that appears catastrophic.

Tension exists between the members of the family because they have opposing reactions to Addie's design. Jewel, her favorite, tightens himself so much that he must release his energy by torturing his horse and cursing. We feel that he cannot be dominated completely by his mother, and his violent outbursts are unconscious acts of rebellion against her authoritarian image. Anse, however, does accept Addie's design because he lacks masculinity. He permits his children to do most of the work, complaining meanwhile about the land. Faulkner captures Anse's submissive need so accurately that we are ready to accept his new marriage as a certainty; like Dostoyevsky's eternal husband, he must marry

---

[1] Robert Penn Warren, "William Faulkner," in *William Faulkner: Two Decades of Criticism*, p. 100.

so that his inadequate ego can, presumably, be dominated by the new Mrs. Bundren. Vardaman and Dewey Dell are also tinged with compulsion. The boy refers to his bloody fish again and again, and it assumes the quality of phobic object for him. So do the buzzards. Dewey Dell, the only woman in the family, is rightly concerned with her pregnancy. All of her musings are about it, and she cannot escape from thinking about it in much the same way as Vardaman does about the fish. Both the fish and the pregnancy become "bigger" than they are.

Unlike the other Bundrens, Darl and Cash try to fight against the design. Darl is the isolated, sensitive being, who cannot remain in an alien mental environment. His first soliloquy shows us how much his mind has been affected by compulsion: he has a precise picture of the road, of the cotton-house in the center of the field, and of the whereabouts of Jewel. The precision is part of his inheritance from Addie. But Darl realizes he must attack this inheritance, and later he sets fire to the barn, hoping that Addie's coffin will be destroyed. Faulkner makes it clear that the act is futile. Cash is a worker more than a thinker. His methodical craftsmanship is recognizable as a kind of compulsion. It is more: it symbolizes a creative pattern formed in the midst of the terrifying world. Cash *endures* because, like Ike McCaslin hunting Old Ben, he concentrates upon creation rather than destruction. His association with the gramophone is symbolic. Cash can work and can listen to music; his life is methodical but also emotional.

Although the reactions of the Bundrens to the design are important, Faulkner introduces other people who have no knowledge of such madness. These people are normal in social terms, although they may be compulsive in limited ways. Cora Tull bases her life upon religious faith, believing that prayer and choral singing are important for getting to Heaven. MacGowan, the druggist's assistant, sees Dewey Dell as an innocent country girl, to whom he can give the treatment in the cellar. Dr. Peabody has a healthy attitude toward death, and he realizes that Anse's inadequacies as a father are destructive to the family group. The reactions of these outsiders make the Bundrens seem more abnormal. When Faulkner opposes the outsiders to the compulsive family intent upon transporting the corpse to Jefferson, the result is horror and grotesque humor.

The opposition of points of view is the crucial structural element of the novel. Faulkner shifts back and forth from members of the family to outsiders, using thought patterns appropriate to each person. His skill is so great that we can identify the character from one sentence. Darl thinks, "*I felt the current take us and I knew we were in the ford by that reason, since it was only by means of that slipping contact that we could tell that we were in motion at all.*" Jewel's thoughts are given only once in the novel: "And now them others [the other Bundrens] sitting there, like buzzards." Anse: "Durn that road." Cash: "It won't balance." Vardaman: "If I jump off the porch I will be where the fish was, and it all cut up into not-fish now." Dewey Dell: "I feel like a wet seed wild in the hot blind earth." Addie Bundren thinks (after she is dead): "My children were of me alone, of the wild blood boiling along the earth, of me and of all that lived; of none and of all." This opposition of points of view is more complex than the chapter juxtapositions in *Light in August*. Faulkner is intent upon portraying family strife, and he uses many points of view toward the one controlling image of design. *As I Lay Dying* has a kaleidoscopic quality because all the Bundrens respond to this same image in strikingly different ways. Addie's soliloquy is static; the other soliloquies fluctuate. We almost respond sympathetically to her rigidity because it occupies this position. It is, to paraphrase Darl, the rim around which the other soliloquies lie like spokes.

Faulkner deliberately opposes movement to the rigidity of the Bundrens even before they begin their journey. The first incident in which the opposition is apparent is that of Jewel and the horse. The entire scene demonstrates how rigidity can compel an individual to explode into violence. Faulkner uses the words "rigid," "motionless," then "spine-jolting jumps." In Jewel's own soliloquy we see him isolating himself with Addie and assaulting the other members of the family. Perhaps the next use of movement occurs when Tull describes Vardaman carrying the fish, which is almost as big as he is. The boy can't control it, and it slides out of his hands. Later he runs about wildly, proclaiming that his mother is (or was) the fish. Dewey Dell's trip to the barn to find Vardaman brings her close to the cows, and she thinks she is the seed "wild in the hot blind earth." Faulkner then describes the preparations for the journey after Addie has actually died. As the coffin is being completed, the drops of rain fall. They are "big as buckshot, warm as though fired from a gun; they sweep across the lantern in a vicious hissing." Cash becomes almost intolerably wet. Then the choral singing begins and Faulkner describes Whitfield and his voice, using the image of two horses swimming across a ford. Carrying the coffin to the wagon, the men almost fall because it isn't balanced properly. Jewel attempts to do most of the work. The coffin "begins to rush away from [Darl] and slip down the air like a sled upon invisible snow, smoothly evacuating atmosphere in which the sense of it is still shaped." Jewel saves it from hitting the ground. Before they leave we see Dewey Dell move into the wagon, "her leg coming long from beneath her tightening dress: that lever which moves the world." The buzzards begin to follow the Bundrens.

Now that the actual journey has begun, Faulkner makes it clear that the road "lies like a spoke of which Addie Bundren is the rim." It is useful to remember Anse's distinction between the road and the traveler:

When He aims for something to be always a-moving, He makes it long ways, like a road or a horse or a wagon, but when He aims for something to stay put, He makes it up-and-down ways, like a tree or a man.

Faulkner presents this opposition in extreme ways. The Bundrens are inflexible; the physical environment appears often to be catastrophic. They will not submit to any part of the environment because of their need to reach Jefferson. Anse, as he sits in the wagon, complains about the "hard country." Samson's soliloquy shows us the Bundrens' reactions—they will continue to move on in the rain, not wanting to eat breakfast. Tull, another outsider whom they meet, realizes that the bridge has fallen. Jewel, however, believes that his family must not wait; he has a mission to perform, and he persuades Anse to agree to cross the river. We are ready for the catastrophe. Darl and Vardaman and Tull supply us with the scene. After Vardaman and Tull express themselves, we ex-

perience an accumulated sense of horror. This feeling is
intensified by the juxtaposition of Cash "lying pole-thin in
his wet clothes. . . ." When the others plunge into the water
to retrieve his tools, Faulkner again emphasizes motion: the
mud is not still. All Cash can do is to lie rigidly, thinking
"It wasn't on a balance."

I have mentioned Addie's soliloquy as occupying an important position in the novel. It occurs now after the water
catastrophe. This is significant because Faulkner wants us
to feel that the Bundrens are still to be influenced by her
design. Motion imagery is used to describe her distinction
between words and doing: words are pictured as going up
in a line and doing goes along the ground. Addie believes in
doing; she is earth-bound. However, we realize that her "doing" is inflexible after a while, and it loses contact with the
natural elements of life. In Whitfield's soliloquy we have
another use of motion imagery—this time the image is associated with his sin (being Jewel's father)—God's hand saves
him from the dangers of the water. When he discovers that
Addie has died, he is relieved that he does not have to confess his sins to the family.

The other catastrophe is the fire. Darl's attempt to destroy
the coffin, to stop the Bundrens, is thwarted by Jewel who,
as soon as the barn becomes red, leaps in to save Addie.
Faulkner is concerned with the terrific energy of Jewel, which
is "compulsive" in nature. This incident compels the other
Bundrens to look upon Darl as a freak. They place him on a
train for Jackson. As he looks out of the train window he
sees the wagon hitched, the mules resting, the other Bundrens
"normal." All the previous violence has ceased. It has been
conquered by the rigidity of the Bundrens, especially Jewel,
who have gone through fire and water, and have doomed
themselves as they have saved Addie.

Like the other critics of As I Lay Dying, I have dwelt
upon the turbulence expressed in scene and image. This is,
however, one force; the other force is rigidity. I would now
like to indicate Faulkner's continual use of images of rigidity,
of nonorganic material, which make us respond to the
compulsive actions of the Bundrens at the same time as we
respond to the violence. The central image is, of course,
Addie's death, which assumes the function of "objective cor-
relative." All the Bundrens are dying because of their rigid-

ity. The novel opens with Darl's precise description of the path. Then we read about Jewel:

Still staring straight ahead, his pale eyes like wood set into his wooden face, he crosses the floor in four strides with the rigid gravity of a cigar-store Indian dressed in patched overalls and endued with life from the hips down.

I think "wood" is particularly important. It is, of course, related to Cash's craftsmanship. Cash, however, has human qualities as he works; he is a pattern-maker who likes "sawing the long hot sad yellow days into planks and nailing them to something." As we read further, Darl again refers to Jewel's eyes looking "like pale wood in his high-blooded face." I believe Faulkner deliberately shows us Darl's awareness of the rigidity about him, especially of Addie's favorite, through his repeated reference to "wooden" Jewel. But other characters think in terms of wood. Through Tull's eyes, Vardaman totes the fish "in both arms like an armful of wood." Tull often uses machinery as an "energetic," nonhuman image. The brain is like "a piece of machinery: it won't stand a whole lot of racking." He implies that this machine should be flexible, not rigid. He thinks of Anse as a "scarecrow" because he realizes instinctively that Anse is not flexible or alive. Anse's "hump" is not alive; Cash's arm, however, moves "in and out of that unhurried imperviousness as a piston moves in the oil."

The images of rigidity increase after the Bundrens begin their journey. Jewel is "wooden-backed" as he sits on his horse. Even Dewey Dell notices that "Jewel sits on his horse like they were both made out of wood, looking straight ahead." As Anse looks at his son Cash, lying rigidly on the ground, he "looks like a figure carved clumsily from tough wood by a drunken caricaturist. It's a trial," he says. When Jewel and Tull attempt to find Cash's tools, they move with "infinitesimal and ludicrous care upon the surface. It looks peaceful, like machinery does after you have watched it and listened to it for a long time." They are expressing their sympathy through work. Cash's broken leg is fixed, ironically enough, by adding cement; he is hurt, imagistically, by rigidity. Addie pictures Anse as a name encompassing a thing without life—like a vessel shaping the liquid flowing into it. In the village Vardaman views the sun as it comes up; he sees "the hill and the mules and the wagon and pa walk on the sun." Jewel's eyes look "like spots of white paper pasted on a high small football." Both images represent a *pasted* pattern, unlike the *shape* of the vessel. The pattern motif is repeated when Jewel struggles with Gillespie, the owner of the barn, as he rushes in to rescue Addie's coffin: "They are like two figures in a Greek frieze, isolated out of all reality by the red glare." Later the buzzards hang, for Darl, "with an outward semblance of form and purpose, but with no inference of motion, progress or retrograde." Faulkner, then, consciously uses the imagery for the last time in the novel when Darl notices the rigidity which has made him a lunatic. The necks of the officers who ride with him to Jackson "were shaved to a hair-line, as though the recent and simultaneous barbers had had a chalk-line like Cash's."

What explains the tone of horror, of grotesque humor? I think it is Faulkner's technique of oppositions. He makes us aware of the rigid principles of the Bundrens and of the natural actions of the world which oppose them. We respond to rigidity so much that we are startled by the movement of fire, water, other human beings. We become accustomed to such procedures as Addie directing her coffin to be built, and we accept them as the "usual." When we encounter Moseley and the river, we become uneasy, wondering whether the rigidity is "usual" and whether the principles of the druggist and the flow of water are "usual." Tension between the two forces makes us anxious, and we laugh. This is Faulkner's intention in *As I Lay Dying*: to make rigidity so vivid that it becomes normal, and to oppose natural movement to the rigidity so that the movement appears catastrophic. The victory of rigidity over movement is horrible. But it is also comic.

The basic technique in *Light in August* is use of the principle of opposition in symbolic relationship to the personal design. When we examine those who possess the rigidity of existence, we seem to consider them in certain groupings: Hightower-Grimm, Burden-Hines, McEachern-Hightower. Percy Grimm is, as I have already indicated, related to Hightower because of the nature of his pathological needs. His design, however, is a violent externalization; the design of Hightower is the abstract product of an introspective personality. This contrast is revealed in the castration scene.

The physical brutality of Grimm is quite unlike the fearful reaction of Hightower when he sees Christmas for the first time. The contrast between designs is also evident in the case of Miss Burden and Doc Hines. Both consider the Negro only as an abstraction, although their standards of behavior differ; Miss Burden looks upon him as a curse, and her pattern is an attempt to placate this curse through humanitarianism—it demonstrates her superstitions and her brooding consciousness; Doc Hines is a man of rage. Like Grimm he does not seem to have the ability to consider the Negro as an object holding a curse over his head. His pattern merely regards him as a harmful force which must be emasculated continually. The contrast, then, between externalized and internalized designs is used by Faulkner to show us that men and women can look for and discover security in various ways. He seems to believe that the hostile defense found through association with the community—as in the case of Grimm's military discipline or Hines's white supremacy—is more dangerous than asocial rigidity because of its destructive influence on the person with the design and on the community itself. We have to remember that Hightower and Miss Burden are considered eccentrics by the people in Jefferson. This is the reason for their seclusion in houses which are referred to as "(that) old Burden house" or the "small brown, almost concealed house" of Hightower. The irony of the situation is that they are separated from the community because *their* inflexibility cannot suffer the inflexibility of their environment.

Investigation of the drives behind these actions leads me to suspect that Faulkner begins with the controlling "image" of design in this novel, and he then proceeds to group his characters in terms of their relation to this "image." Richard Chase cannot understand the need for "the episodes of family and cultural history which accompany Faulkner's account of Miss Burden and Hightower."[2] His statement is interesting because it reveals the fact that we must look at the personal design before we can integrate successfully those parts of *Light in August* which appear trivial or obscure. We have to know about their family backgrounds before we can under-

    [2] Richard Chase, "The Stone and the Crucifixion: Faulkner's *Light in August*," in *William Faulkner: Two Decades of Criticism*, p. 215.

stand the reasons for Miss Burden's and Hightower's desires
to develop authoritarian patterns of behavior. We have to
realize that they *do* act strangely because of their need to
escape from incidents (like the sickness of Hightower's parents or the deaths of Miss Burden's ancestors) whose implications they refused to grasp. Both the Hightower-Grimm
and Hines-Burden relationships are apparent only when the
similar insecure needs are studied. I believe that one reason
for the failure of the reader to notice the symbolic resem-
blance of these people is their isolation (both spatial and
temporal) from each other. Faulkner wants to suggest to us
that each design is so personalized that it can remove the
power of communication from people who share the desire
for certainty in life.

The sexual impotence of the father is stressed in *Light
in August*. His compulsions are individualized to such a
point of cold abstractionism that he refuses to leave the self
behind or to extend the self outward to consider a woman's
need for affection. The father believes that love is dangerous
because it implies the search for new meaning. Faulkner
realizes that this inadequacy of the father is connected with
his inability to recognize his son and to pity him. The acknowledgment of a filial bond can be real only if there is a
strength of will which can permit the father to look objec-
tively at his own immobility and to see it as the sign of inhumanity. This seems to be impossible. Love of woman and
pity for son require the capacity of the father to stand alone
with an awareness of the emotional needs which cannot be
satisfied by an obsessive design.

When he has to deliver Lena's child, Hightower cannot
obtain complete satisfaction because he realizes his own lack
of a namesake. His impassivity in thwarting his wife's desires
has alienated him from the "*good stock peopling in tranquil
obedience to it the good earth.*" Unlike Hightower, McEachern, the Calvinist, has definite ideas about the woman. He
cannot appreciate her fertility because he can only consider
her an object of disgust and filth which the Lord created out
of necessity. Eve and Jezebel, the harlot, are equated in his
mind. It is ironic that he is forced to adopt Joe as his son
because of his own impotence, and he is able to find some
sort of sexual pleasure through the torture (brutal whipping)
of this son. In the final scene of the novel Percy Grimm gains

satisfaction from making Joe as unmanly as he is. His sadism is a perverse libidinal outlet, demonstrating the fact that he cannot engage in normal intercourse.

The rebellion of Christmas against those people who have authoritarian patterns is easily seen. His experience with other characters is not limited as in the case of Hightower, Miss Burden, and McEachern, who live away from social violence. His range of experience is great because Faulkner wants to show Christmas constantly searching for the meaning of his humanity. His rebellion against the society which has twisted his personality is seen, then, in terms of representative associations with at least five other people. The ambivalence of Christmas as the son is manifest in his sexual plight. ⁴His relation to the male can never be satisfactory because he desires the authoritarian force of the male, the substitute father-image, and he wants to destroy this force at the same time, realizing that he is lacking it.⁴ He is as aware of his own unformed masculinity in his mid-thirties as he was in his youthful adventures with McEachern. It is characteristic that the Sabbath whipping was pleasurable to Joe; he wanted to yield to the strength of the black-suited farmer in a particularly passive way. But this could not afford total release. Christmas still wanted to define his manhood by means of intercourse (in the same way that Miss Burden wanted to become a woman in the affair), and his attempts to find confidence with the prostitutes he visited, especially the Negro ones, were unsuccessful. He is afraid of the woman because he believes unconsciously that her behavior is an unnatural consequence of her malfunctioning as a man. He sees her, in other words, as an image of the castration which he both loathes and desires: "It was the woman: that soft kindness which he believed himself doomed to be forever victim of and which he hated worse than the hard and ruthless justice of men." The father commands more respect from Joe. Faulkner does not go as far as Freud did in *Totem and Taboo* to demonstrate the "truth" that the Oedipus complex—for this is essentially Joe's plight—is the origin of all social behavior. But he does try to present the rootlessness of the son in quest of his own identity in terms which are relevant to our times. We read the tale of Christmas with terror because we see that he is not only trapped by his noncommunicative state between two races—he cannot communicate with any other person (male or female) in the entire world. The problem of his latent homosexuality is therefore an apt symbol in the social context.

It may seem to the reader that Lena is also associated with the road. But unlike Christmas she is sure and peaceful in her search. Her destination is marriage. Her range of experience is restricted to those people who can help her find the "real" father of her child, her prospective husband, and the people who assist her in childbirth. Lena is a distinct presence in the community of violence. She learns about the horror of Jefferson from Byron Bunch, and she begins to sense in her simple way that this man is not violent like the other citizens she hears about. Faulkner uses Byron Bunch in the novel as an important link between the world of personal design and the world of nature. He is more than a disinterested spectator, a confidant, who supplies necessary information to both Lena and Hightower about Christmas and the murder of Miss Burden. His point of view is unique. He must choose to continue his twilight conversations with Hightower or to accept his growing attachment to Lena Grove. In the novel his fumbling movements are the manifestations of an internal dilemma. Hightower hears him "stumble heavily at the dark bottom step" throughout the early chapters. After Byron does accept the fact that he must help Lena and abandon his spiritual guide, he walks erect in a different way. In Chapter 13 Faulkner writes: "Tonight Byron is completely changed. It shows in his walk, his carriage; leaning forward Hightower says to himself *As though he has learned pride or defiance.* . . . 'He has done something. He has taken a step.' "

If we realize the significance of Faulkner's sexual presentation of the themes of rigidity and rebellion in *Light in August,* we can see the importance of the union of Byron and Lena. Byron Bunch is identified throughout the novel as the friend of Hightower. His enthusiastic acceptance of Hightower's ideas until the entrance of Lena indicates that he is to be as susceptible to the code as Miss Burden was to the one of her ancestors. The statement he makes about Hightower is also characteristic of his own feelings before he meets her: ". . . a fellow is more afraid of the trouble he might have than he ever is of the trouble he's already got. He'll cling to trouble he's used to before he'll risk a change."

But Faulkner uses their relationship to suggest that Byron, although he has potentialities for a compulsive retreat into rigid doctrine, is, nevertheless, able to understand the inadequacies which the personal design represents. Byron realizes that Hightower is unable to break through his pattern to help Lena. Byron's own developing awareness of her is parallel to his refusal to accept the abstractionism of Hightower. He moves her into the cabin in spite of the fact that they are not yet married; he realizes that his own sense of morality is more important to Lena and himself than the gossip of other people. Faulkner shows us Byron's ability to see the importance of motherhood. The newborn son is more valid than "dead" Hightower. It does not matter that Byron cannot employ strength in his battle with Lucas Burch. His vision of the world has increased tremendously. His involvement with the woman has given him an insight into the differences—and the opportunity to choose—between right and wrong, justice and injustice. The pastoral ending suggests to us that his further association with her will help him to see more of the fecundity of nature which he could easily have forgotten. As they ride away from Jefferson, Byron Bunch and Lena Grove look at the fields and the sky. He now knows the meaning of love; she knows that he is to be a "real" father to her child. Man and woman seem to be at one with nature.

The opposition of points of view is used by Faulkner in chapter juxtapositions to give us a sense of strife. This is quite effective in the last three chapters. Chapter 19 has external brutality because it concerns the final attempt of Christmas to gain recognition at Hightower's house. Percy Grimm and his men enter in pursuit. Christmas is viewed from the outside, and his death possesses a certain quality of purity and greatness as a result of this objectivity. In this chapter the rhythms used by Faulkner come to rest after the swiftness of the pursuit, as Christmas discovers in death the only certainty he has ever known. Chapter 20 concerns the reverie of Hightower. It begins slowly so as not to disturb the tone of the crucifixion scene. Faulkner stresses the cumulative effect of his mental associations. We see from the rhythm, however, that the state of his mind is no longer tranquil. His thinking is now a wheel gathering momentum. The rush of the pursuit of Christmas has become the rush of approaching madness which overwhelms Hightower. This chapter ends not with rest but with the frenzy of the past he had wanted to embrace so much. Chapter 21 is, of course, different. Faulkner shows us Lena and Byron in a rural setting. They can flee from the ravaged community into the country, where there is no confusion of mind. The dialogue—which, perhaps, stresses human communication—of the chapter is comic, and as natural as everyday occurrence. The dialect of the narrator, a traveling furniture dealer, catches the calm quality of the scene when Lena looks out from his wagon: "Just sitting there, riding, looking out like she hadn't ever seen country—roads and trees and fields and telephone poles—before in her life." Lena has completed the journey she began. She can enjoy the ride in the wagon with Byron and her child because she is *satisfied*.

Faulkner uses the face-to-face scenes of these characters with dissimilar points of view in *Light in August* to achieve a quality of tension we usually associate with drama. And the meeting with another outlook involves a process which offers enlightenment to at least one of the characters. It must be emphasized that the flight of Christmas to Hightower's house is a necessary part of the plot. Their confrontation produces tension, and the symbolic conflict of the father and the son is revealed in the tumult of this scene. Christmas turns upon Hightower, who could have helped him to realize his identity. He knows, although he cannot express it verbally, that Hightower's rigidity cannot permit him to offer recognition to any person. Hightower, on the other hand, realizes that the compulsive standards of behavior which he adopted in the past have destroyed his power to act, and this realization is responsible, as I have mentioned, for his madness. The visit of Hightower to the cabin where Lena is staying is dramatic because both characters belong again to two essentially different ways of life. Their convergence, however, is not physical. Hightower recognizes his own impotence for the first time when he looks down at the child he has helped to deliver. The style, of his own thought in retrospect, is suggestive of his grave despair: "*That child that I delivered. I have no namesake. But I have known them before this to be named by a grateful mother for*

the doctor who officiated." There is not any confrontation
of Christmas and Lena in the novel. Nevertheless the son
does come close to what the pregnant woman actually represents. He is tired by his unsuccessful wanderings; he cannot
continue to destroy or be destroyed. Christmas gains a new
understanding of the fertility which he can never embrace
as his movements come to a halt in the forest before his death.
The serenity of the style is appropriate:

> It is as though he desires to see the native earth in all its phases
> for the first or the last time. . . . For a week now he has lurked
> and crept among its secret places. For some time as he walks
> steadily on, he thinks that this is what it is—the looking and the
> seeing—which gives him peace and unhaste and quiet . . .

But the feeling cannot last. We see him again only when he
attacks Hightower and Grimm.

Faulkner uses the principle of temporal opposition in the
same way that he uses the chapter juxtapositions I have been
tracing. His temporal form is indicative of his treatment of
the three major characters. Chapter 3 demonstrates Faulkner's presentation of time in regard to Hightower throughout
the novel. We see him in the present, sitting at the window
as twilight approaches. Our knowledge of his history comes
as Faulkner—after he is sure that we do not lose our first
impression—shifts backward in time, using Byron, an outsider, to describe this past. The chapter then ends when
Hightower sees Byron approach the house. Faulkner seems
to want to bring him back to our times in order to allude to
the contrast between his reverie, which is devoted to remote
events, and events which occur now. Hightower may hope
to relive the life of his grandfather, but his creator refuses to
give more than minor exposition of his own history and the
history of the general. The contrast between his reverie (of
past experiences) and his inaction (seen in the present tense)
is effectively used to give an understanding of the failure of
Hightower as a man of action.

The wheel which Hightower sees in his mind is important
as a symbol. The wheel, a Jungian mandala, is representative
of the continuum. Hightower has not been able to realize this
flow of life until now because he has tried to freeze time.
After he observes the castration of Christmas, he realizes,
however, that horrible, meaningful things occur in the pres-

ent, that the continuum cannot be ordered by the mental
processes of man. It is too late. The wheel, which is destructive to his own rigid personality, points the way to madness.

Faulkner believes that Christmas was corrupted in the
past before he was able to discover himself. He was formed
by outside influences. Why does he distrust Miss Burden in
the affair? Why does he rebel in the church? Why does he
refuse to accept his status as either Negro or white until the
day of his death? Christmas cannot answer these questions;
he cannot relate his complex remote experiences which make
him act as he does. He cannot comprehend that his psycho-
pathic tendencies as an adult are a result of his inability to
gain childhood love. This point of view of Christmas is indicated by the temporal form. Chapter 5, which concerns his
confusion before the murder of Miss Burden, ends with:
"*Something is going to happen. Something is going to happen to me . . .*" It is noteworthy that Faulkner does not
place a period at the end of the sentence. He then presents
an exposition of five chapters extending in time from Joe's
experiences in the orphanage until his arrival in Jefferson.
This sudden emergence of past events suggests to us that
Christmas cannot have a reasonable view of the present. His
mind is dominated by the early experiences which warped
his personality. Unlike Hightower he does not try consciously to recapture the past through reverie. His awareness of it comes suddenly when the places and events he has
tried to repress demand expression—they overcome the years
of censorship and rush into his consciousness. Faulkner is
able to condense Christmas' sense into one paragraph at the
beginning of Chapter 6. We see here his tortured failure to
understand the early pattern of his life, his simple hate and
fear which cannot be relinquished. But his past is simply
unconsciously responsible for his present actions. It continues to demand expression in thought processes, but he cannot conceptualize the horrible meaning; he is unable to relate
the ugly experiences to his personality. A conscious awareness of these incidents would probably give him a clearer
notion of his own need for love, which has led to wild and
bitter actions.

Faulkner believes that Lena has the most adequate conception of time. The present moment holds concrete reality
for her. Her faith allows her to act spontaneously toward

events while they are occurring. The present is the necessary link between past events (which can be used to interpret it) and future events (which it can help predict). Faulkner again stresses his point of view toward Lena through his form. He considers her adventures in the very first chapter because he wants us to see her as nature before we see the conflict of the father and the son. Her journey is described almost entirely in the present tense, which emphasizes her concern with the immediate event in contrast to the event of the past, Lucas Burch's flight, the cause of her wandering. But Faulkner shows us that Lena, while acting spontaneously, senses the fact that she has a goal—marriage—in the future. The vital interrelation of three aspects of time is, therefore, emphasized in Chapter 1. This is not found either in the chapters which concern Hightower or in those which concern Christmas. Even the imagery strengthens the totality of her conception of time. We read that she moves on the road as "slow, deliberate, unhurried and tireless as augmenting afternoon itself . . ."; her journey has "all the peaceful and monotonous changes between darkness and day." Faulkner demonstrates that the actions of Lena are gradual because they reflect in their continuity the actual changes in the outside world. Her own cycle (symbolized by menstruation) is in accord with the cycle of the seasons, the days, the flow of past into present into future. Faulkner extends this implication in the last chapter of the novel. We see Lena on the road after the turbulence in Hightower's house has ended. He forces us to remember our first impression of her and to compare it to our present impression. We see one significant change—she is now with Byron Bunch. She *has* reached her destination because she has been able to realize the inescapable vitality of the present in contrast to the formed past and the not-yet-formed future. Faulkner suggests to us that Lena Grove is aware of the importance of time as a wheel which moves in a slow but sure way as she travels in its circle. Her wheel—unlike Hightower's—is the symbol of completion during movement.

    Richard Chase believes that the texture of *Light in August* is "very much a matter of mechanics and dynamics—a poetry of physics."[3] His statement does take into account some of

---

[3] *Ibid.*, p. 205.

the various oppositions—although he does not completely understand the technique—I have described. Faulkner, however, is more than a physicist. His novels are not to be charted and explained as sets of scientific formulae. The value of his technique of opposition would be lost were the oppositions not concretized in myth. His vision *is* vital because he does associate design with the father, rebellion against the design with the son, nature with the woman. The line and curve images Chase sees are merely the result of Faulkner's identification of the line and the curve with his mythic representatives. The male is the line because of his rigid, powerful standards, his phallus. The female is the curve because of her cyclical movement demonstrated by menstruation. Chase seems to have the same sort of association. He believes that Christmas gashes the whisky tins (the curve image) to find "something liquid, death colored, and foul." But actually Christmas sees this liquid in his mind only after he listens to a graphic description of her cycle by the prostitute, Bobbie Allen, who, as Faulkner writes, "[used] the only words she knew perhaps." It is the distrust of the woman which makes him see the liquid flow from the cracked urns in a kind of dream. It seems, then, as if Chase also associates the woman with the curve image (the urn).

In his essay "Technique as Discovery" Mark Schorer writes: "Technique is the means by which the writer's experience, which is his subject matter, compels him to attend to it; technique is the only means he has of discovering, exploring, developing his subject, of conveying its meaning and finally of evaluating it."[4] The study of Faulkner's technique in *Light in August* has substantiated, I believe, my conception of his theme. His employment of oppositions of points of view indicates that he is concerned with the conflict of personalities in our times. Meetings of characters, as of Hightower and Lena—although coupled with illumination of personal deficiencies—generate more tension. His temporal juxtapositions suggest that Christmas and Hightower do not have a clear understanding of the situations of the present, because one is dominated by the release of pent-up hate, and the other is stifled by a conscious attempt to hold remote

[4] Mark Schorer, "Technique as Discovery," in *Critiques and Essays in Modern Fiction, 1920–1951, ed. John W. Aldridge* (New York: Ronald Press, 1952), p. 67.

glory. Consequently they cannot cope with the problems which beset them. Where can flexibility be found? Where can order be found? How can the two be combined to give us meaning and enjoyment? Faulkner seems to imply by his first and last chapters that we must find completion in the world of Lena. Strife should make us return to those commonplace experiences which offer serenity and beauty in life. But the reader cannot identify himself completely with Lena; she is seen as an idealized person, unaware of the very important conflict in the male world. Like Faulkner, he becomes too involved with the rigidity of the father and the rebellion of the son to more than glance at her. He is more impressed with the greater portions of *Light in August* which concern Joe's need to fight against the infamy of codes which distort his *Weltanschauung*—scenes likes the one between Christmas and McEachern at the dance hall; between Christmas and Miss Burden when she tries to save his soul; between Christmas and Hightower. I believe that the technique of Faulkner is, therefore, appropriate because by it he suggests that he is terrified by these compulsions which cast the curse upon both the father and the son. He can offer only a fleeting vision of the cyclical resolution of opposites in *Light in August*.

FAULKNER AND THE BIBLE

5

FAULKNER AND THE BIBLE

In reply to interviewers' questions about his reading, Faulkner frequently cites the Old Testament as one of his favorite books. This is significant because many of his critics have hinted at the biblical, the legalistic, elements in his work. In this chapter I would like to indicate the uses Faulkner makes of the Bible, particularly the Old Testament, for his imagery and, what is much more important, for his themes.

Perhaps the simplest way of demonstrating Faulkner's reliance upon and knowledge of the Bible is to list some of the allusions encountered in his work:

New Testament

Jesus, mentioned in *Mirrors of Chartres Street* (p. 2), *Soldiers' Pay* (p. 319), *The Sound and the Fury* (p. 311), *Light in August* (throughout the novel), *Absalom, Absalom!* (p. 198), *Go Down, Moses* (p. 309), *Requiem for a Nun* (p. 163), *A Fable* (throughout the novel).

Golgotha (Calvary), the site of Jesus' crucifixion, mentioned in *The Wild Palms* (p. 264).

Nazareth, the birthplace of Jesus, used as part of the title of one of the articles Faulkner contributed to the New Orleans *Times-Picayune*, "Out of Nazareth."

Old Testament

The Old Testament found by name in *Go Down, Moses* (p. 371). Genesis, however, is mentioned in both *The Wild Palms* (p. 232) and *Requiem for a Nun* (p. 48).

Lilith, the mysterious woman before Eve, named in *The Wild Palms* (p. 115), *Requiem for a Nun* (p. 260), and *A Fable* (p. 153). I can find one reference to Adam and Eve in *Sanctuary* (p. 181).

Isaac supplies the name of the wise old man, Ike Mc-Caslin, in "The Bear" and other stories of *Go Down, Moses* (p. 279).

Benjamin, the youngest son of Jacob, mentioned throughout *The Sound and the Fury* and in *Go Down, Moses* (p. 371).

Moses, the lawgiver, mentioned in the title story of *Go Down, Moses.*

The Ten Commandments. "Thou Shalt Not Kill" is specifically used by Gavin Stevens in *Intruder in the Dust* (p. 200).

Canaan, the land "flowing with milk and honey," mentioned in *Go Down, Moses* (p. 279).

Jordan, mentioned by the Negroes in *The Unvanquished* (p. 115).

David. His friendship with Jonathan is mentioned in *Mirrors of Chartres Street* (p. 37).

Absalom, the rebellious son, used symbolically throughout the novel *Absalom, Absalom!*

Although this list is far from exhaustive, we can learn several things from it: (1) Faulkner is very much interested in the figure of Christ; he has used Christ more often than other persons or incidents. (2) The Old Testament, however, supplies a greater amount of material than does the New Testament. (3) References to the Bible range from citations of single lines to the use of symbolic people throughout entire novels. (4) Faulkner frequently uses biblical allusions to suggest that his characters and incidents are not merely contemporary—they have traditional elements which, although undeveloped, give them importance and timelessness not apparent at first sight. One example will suffice here. In "Out of Nazareth" Faulkner writes about a young man looking at a cathedral:

Hatless, his young face brooded upon the spire of the Cathedral, or perhaps it was something in the sky he was watching. Beside him was a small pack; leaning against his leg was a staff.

. . . And one could imagine young David looking like that. One could imagine Jonathan getting that look from David, and, serving that highest function of which sorry man is capable, being the two of them beautiful in similar peace and simplicity—beautiful as gods, as no woman could ever be.

By means of the biblical imagery we begin to accept the fact that the youth is not simply a wanderer in a dingy New Orleans street, that he has, in fact, spiritual potentialities which he can develop, can make manifest, to achieve happiness. But the Bible can also be referred to ironically, as in *Sanctuary*. When Temple thinks about female sex appeal, she wonders whether women are, perhaps, more attractive dressed than nude. She remembers her girl friend saying that the Snake noticed Eve only after Adam "made her put on a fig leaf." The sudden intrusion of this image indicates Faulkner's belief that Temple does not regard the Bible as a source of religious wisdom—indeed, she has the fall of man in mind because it can help her to "prove" an unimportant point about sex.

More important than these allusions is Faulkner's reliance upon biblical themes—the father-son relationship being one. This close relationship of the father and the son is evident in the Old Testament description of the lives of Abraham, Isaac, and Jacob. It was expected that the son would obey the father, would follow in his footsteps in the same way all the tribes followed the celestial Father. The anthropomorphic representation of God indicates that the Hebrews believed the structure of the family was, in essence, the structure of the universe. Rebellion against the father was unheard of because it was a mortal sin. The patriarchal tradition was so much a part of Hebraic culture that it occurs in the prophets of the Exile, and it is still present in the beliefs of contemporary Jews (for instance, it is usually much more difficult for Jewish parents to accept a daughter as the first-born child than a son).

In the first two chapters I have tried to indicate that Faulkner is so concerned with the theme of rigidity that he creates his own myth of father and son to establish it in human terms. In his novels he is employing the method of ancient writers. The Hebrews (and the Greeks) suggested problems of universal importance in their literature through the consideration of father-son relationships. Faulkner believes that these stories embody traditional values, "the old universal truths lacking which any story is ephemeral and doomed." He realizes that these values of duty, of justice, of love, are not as prevalent as they once were. He believes that he can contrast his father-son relationships to those of ancient writers, that he can use parallels between the two to give us a sense of the differences between past and present values.

Faulkner uses the Old Testament relationship of Absalom and David. In II Samuel, Absalom, the son of David, is the most beautiful creature in the land of Israel, and he is loved by his father and all of his friends. But Absalom has an abundance of pride, which compels him to expect more than this universal acclaim. He wants as much regal power as his father. Absalom rebels against David, and he is slain in battle after his hair is caught in the branches of an oak. His father can only weep when he hears the news. He realizes the nature of Absalom's pride, but he can, nevertheless, acknowledge the fact of his blood tie to his rebellious son through this lament: "O my son Absalom, my son, my son Absalom! would God I had died for thee, O Absalom, my son, my son!" In his novel *Absalom, Absalom!* Faulkner concentrates upon the description of Bon's inadequacies in the eyes of Thomas Sutpen to show us that this father cannot even regard his son as human, let alone beautiful. Unlike the biblical Absalom, Bon rebels because he wants to be granted the recognition of this humanity; his rebellion is not the result of overweening pride. Also, the blood mixture of Bon in Faulkner's myth is equated with the hair of Absalom—it is the agent of destruction. This is evident in the incidents between Sutpen and Bon. The differences, however, are again revealing. The Negro blood of the mulatto is not his fault. It is the necessary consequence of Sutpen's illicit union with an octoroon mistress in New Orleans. Faulkner understands that the values inherent in the lament of David are now lost. Sutpen cannot have a new vision of any personal inadequacies which forced Bon to rebel (in the way David can, although, in the biblical story, he is not basically at fault). He can only continue to obey his design and rebuild his empire in the same way that he did before—and, ironically, he even tries to father another illegitimate son. This action is responsible for his own death at the hands of Wash Jones.

Faulkner uses the Christ symbol in *Light in August*. He concentrates upon the plight of Christmas as the result of his conflict with a society composed of individuals with personal designs. I believe that Faulkner uses the association of Joe with Christ—indicated by such details as the age (thirty-three), the betrayal by Lucas Burch (Judas), the facts of his mysterious birth—to suggest that the son dies for a heroic cause. He is crucified because he tries to assert the integrity of the individual, whether he realizes this or not. This is clearly seen in the death scene. His blood "seemed to rush out of his pale body like the rush of sparks from a rising rocket; upon that black blast the man seemed to rise soaring into their memories forever and ever." The resurrection of Christ in the Bible is equated with the living memory Joe can offer to those who learn about his plight. But Faulkner also uses the Christ symbol in an ironic way. He believes that the son is unable to fight corruption with love because he has never known kindness, or pity, or love from his father-image. He has learned only to destroy or to be destroyed. In this respect Faulkner seems consciously to distort the words of Christ at the Last Supper: "As the Father hath loved me, so have I loved you: continue ye in my love. If ye keep my commandments, ye shall abide in my love; even as I have kept my Father's commandments, and abide in His love." There is, to be sure, martyrdom in the novel. The martyrdom comes after the turbulent rebellion against the father. Faulkner's ambiguous use of the Christ symbol is forceful because it shows that the traditional elements of Christian love and charity are frequently absent in our times. The father cannot love because of the pride which compels him to seek certainty through design; the son cannot love because he has learned the meaning of violence from the father. The violence of Christmas, therefore, opposes the violence of the society which has corrupted him. In short, he fights with hate for a noble cause.

Of course, Faulkner uses the Christ symbol in *A Fable*. In the novel the Corporal is equated with Christ, and he is forced to undergo the same experiences, which include temptation in the wilderness, the last supper, the crucifixion, and the resurrection. In *A Fable* Faulkner cannot achieve the same tense, ambiguous effect with his symbolism which he had in *Light in August*. He is too concerned with tracing distinct similarities rather than ironic contrasts. The Corporal is passive and almost noncommital in his mutiny; he is a shadowy figure who observes rather than acts. He is seen "as in a glass darkly" because Faulkner wants us to feel that the other characters have merely an inkling of the true worth of his humanity and divinity. When the Corporal does speak, we do not expect crudeness of speech—indeed, we are alarmed to hear his voice because we have become accustomed to seeing him from afar, as we did at the beginning of the novel, as he stands in the truck which brings him to the prison. We question the latest use of the Christ symbol because we cannot suppose the Corporal to be both a soldier and a pacifist. Our sensibilities are shaken. How can Christ be a military man? How are we to believe in the palpable reality of the Corporal if we are so conscious that he *is* Christ? In other words, are we reading about Christ or the Corporal? In *Light in August* we believed in the reality of Christmas and *then* in his symbolic value, feeling that more was suggested than was easily apparent. The Corporal, however, remains a symbol which stands in the distance rather than becoming an actual human being like Christmas. In a sense we—like Faulkner—must view him as a dim Platonic recollection which we can learn to comprehend fully only in the future.

Faulkner uses the story of the "sacrifice" of Isaac by Abraham with subtlety. In the Old Testament, Abraham, the first patriarch of the Hebrews, who had entered into a "mutually exclusive agreement with God, whereby he was to recognize and worship no other deity and God was to protect and seek the welfare of Abraham and his family . . . ,"[1] is commanded one day by God to take his son, Isaac, to an altar and slay him. Actually this is to be a test of Isaac's obedience to Abraham and, in turn, of Abraham's obedience to the Father. The two prove their allegiance through the preparations for the ritual, and the son does not have to die. He and Abraham both learn that God is merciful and benevolent toward those who love Him. The biblical ritual ends: "And Abraham lifted up his eyes, and looked, and behold behind *him* a ram caught in a thicket by his horns: and Abraham went and took the ram, and offered him for a burnt offering in the stead of his son." I have already described the nature of the Sam Fathers–Isaac McCaslin relationship. It is quite evident that Faulkner chooses the name Isaac to suggest reli-

[1] Harry Orlinsky, *Ancient Israel* (Ithaca, New York: Cornell University Press, 1954), p. 28.

gious associations in much the same way that Crane does with his symbolism in *The Red Badge of Courage.* "The Bear" stresses the submission of the son (Isaac) to the priest (Sam-Abraham) and of both the priest and the sacrificial victim to the wilderness. The hunt for the bear, which is part of the wilderness, is dangerous because it involves conflict. It is true that Sam, as Abraham, prepares Isaac for the hunt, but it is Sam's *covenant* with Old Ben, and with the trees—in short, with the awe-inspiring wilderness about him—which is at the heart of the story. Unfortunately, Faulkner means to imply that the happy ending no longer exists. He realizes that the blood relationship of Sam Fathers and Isaac McCaslin cannot last in our times. The death of the spiritual father is intertwined with the murder of Old Ben by Boon Hogganbeck. Man and animal were one in the past. They were both representatives of the old order in which humility could be sought by this entry into strife. Old Ben taught Sam Fathers to search for the wildness of nature and to tame it, in order to gain a clear understanding of the potentialities of the human spirit. This is what Isaac was able to learn from his father; but he alone lives on in "The Bear" to see the total ruin of the wilderness which was their temple. He witnesses the arrival of the lumber company machines. He realizes that modern men of commerce are concerned not with the preparation for spiritual understanding but with material gain.

The idea of a covenant in Faulkner's work is, like his emphasis upon the father-son relationship, related to the Old Testament. Abraham's agreement with the Lord which I have just mentioned was renewed, in turn, by Isaac and Jacob—He became "the Kinsman of Isaac" and the "Champion of Jacob"—but the Covenant between all the Hebrews and God came into existence during the period of Moses. The exodus from Egypt into the Promised Land, Canaan, with the giving of the Ten Commandments on Mount Sinai, indicated that He was now on the side of the entire nation. The personal agreement developed, then, into a distinct social reality—the Hebrews became the Chosen People. Faulkner believes that the South must accept the significance of a mutual agreement or bond not only between particular Negroes and white men, but between the region and destiny (the North, the land, and the will of God). The idea of the covenant, both personal and social, is an important aspect of his work, giving much of it a legalistic tone.

In *The Unvanquished* Faulkner gives us a lengthy description of the two brothers, Buck and Buddy McCaslin. They are unique in the novel because of their ideas of social relationship. Both of them believe that all people—slave, white trash, and plantation owner—belong to the land, that there is an agreement between themselves and the earth which they farm. Like the Hebrew patriarchs, they affirm this covenant to be a moral influence upon their subsequent actions:

They believed . . . that the earth would permit them to live on and out of it and use it only so long as they behaved and that if they did not behave right, it would shake them off just like a dog getting rid of fleas.

Consequently Buck and Buddy are able to respect the Negro, permitting their slaves to earn their freedom by working the land. Of course this kind of covenant opposes the design of men like Sartoris. Faulkner sympathizes with the Utopianism or, if you will, the communistic ideal, of the brothers while realizing that it is doomed. Most Southerners during the Civil War and the Reconstruction are too intent upon self-centered capitalism to consider a new economic relationship which threatens their wealth and security. In *The Unvanquished* the defeat of Buck and Buddy is indicated not only by the glorification of Sartoris' design by people like Drusilla and Rosa Millard, but by an incident in which only one of the brothers, Buddy, is permitted to join the Confederate Army to help save the homeland. Sartoris (and what he represents) re-emerges, then, as the powerful force. Faulkner believes, nevertheless, in the inspirational qualities of these two brothers, who can father a Covenant for the South, even though they themselves are bachelors.

The covenant theme, with important variations, is repeated in "The Bear." Part Four, Isaac's rhetorical conversation with his cousin, stresses the idea that the entire South, not merely a Buck or Buddy, is bound to the land; the isolated covenant in *The Unvanquished* is expanded here until it assumes cosmic proportions. Isaac realizes the nature of the agreement (because of his ritual with Sam-Abraham) and provokes the anger of his cousin (a believer in the de-

sign). Isaac believes that He entered into a covenant with
Southerners, teaching them the necessity of reorientation
after the War, the need to abide by freedom for the slaves
and for the earth itself. His countrymen did not heed the
warnings, the Commandments, and they are now suffering
the wrath of God. But the Negroes, who have understood
the goodness of the land and the higher teachings of the
Bible, can help them to lift this "curse." Isaac McCaslin believes, therefore, in the recognition of a universal Covenant,
a set of laws, to which all men, black and white, must aspire
in order to save their land, their country, and themselves. His
own strength is evident when he says, "I am free." McCaslin
Edmonds, his cousin, senses that this is not pure talk, that
Isaac is truly a believer in the equality of men. He says,

'Chosen, I suppose (I will concede it) out of all your time by
Him as you say Buck and Buddy were from theirs. And it took
Him a bear and an old man and four years just for you. And it
took you fourteen years to reach that point and about that many,
maybe more for Old Ben, and more than seventy for Sam Fathers.
And you are just one. How long then? How long?' and he
'It will be long. I have never said otherwise.'

In *Intruder in the Dust* Gavin Stevens (who is translating
the Old Testament into classic Greek) realizes the importance of the covenant, but I think his conception differs from
those of Buck and Buddy and Isaac. Gavin Stevens believes
that the South must see itself as a homogeneous unit, apart
from the diverse elements of the rest of the country. It must
save itself in practical situations. Negroes like Lucas Beauchamp must be treated as equals, like business partners or
covenant holders. Faulkner suggests the nature of this kind
of bond at the end of the novel. For the services he has ren-
dered, Gavin Stevens accepts the Negro's money; Lucas asks
for a receipt. Actually Faulkner is saying that such transactions should occur not only in law offices but in buses,
schools, and movie houses. Lucas and the white man, working together, present a united front against "the spurious up-
roar" of the second-best elements in both the South and the
North—indeed, the North is often the enemy to be watched,
an enemy intent upon quick, superficial freedom for everyone and no one. Clearly the social consciousness here is akin
to the strong feeling of the Hebrews as a chosen unit in the

face of conflict and oppression. But the Chosen in the South remain few.

The kinship of the Hebrews and Negroes is apparent in Faulkner's work. Both peoples have an extreme devotion to the Lord, believing they are tested daily and affirming their qualities of endurance. Like the Hebrews in bondage in Egypt or, later, in Babylonia, the Negroes have their faith to uphold them in a land of infidels (which include ardent Calvinists like Miss Burden). It is, of course, significant that more biblical allusions to captivity occur in *Go Down, Moses*, which deals mainly with the Negroes, than in the other novels. The title story presents this kinship of Hebrew and Negro. Molly Beauchamp, an aged Negress, worries constantly about her grandson who has left his homeland. She does not know that he is a criminal, a horrible product of black and white relations, that he is to be executed for murder. But she does think of him as Benjamin, a captive in a foreign land: "Sold him in Egypt. I dont know whar he is. I just knows Pharoh got him. And you the Law. I wants to find my boy." As he does in *Intruder in the Dust*, Gavin Stevens, the lawyer, tries to help the Negro: this time he collects—and contributes—money to bring the corpse of the "slain wolf" back to Mississippi. His action is symbolic of the acknowledgment of the white man's debt to the Negro. In *The Unvanquished* we have the same kind of identification. During the War a group of Negroes tries to flee from slave territory. Faulkner considers them engaged in an Exodus from the South into the Promised Land, Canaan, and he describes them sympathetically in one of his great mob scenes (another such scene occurs at the end of *A Fable*) as they try to reach and cross the River Jordan.

One of the powerful sermons in literature is found in *The Sound and the Fury*. Dilsey, the old Negress, and Benjy Compson, the thirty-three-year-old idiot, go to church on Easter morning. Faulkner suggests that this symbolic action separates them from the decay of the Compson household, because they have religious fervor. Of course the idiot's name is chosen to show that he—like the Negro—is an outcast in the South. Benjy and Dilsey, however, see more goodness and evil about them than do Jason, the materialist, Mrs. Compson, the neurasthenic mother, and Uncle Maury. By concentrating his energies upon the Negro preacher in this scene, Faulkner is able to demonstrate that these two people, idiot and Negress, are united in spiritual wisdom as they sit and listen to the words of the preacher:

"When de long, cold—Oh, I tells you, Breddren, when de long, cold—I sees de light en I sees de word, po sinner! Dey passed away in Egypt, de swingin chariots; de generations passed away. Was a rich man: whar he now O breddren? Was a po man: whar he now O sistuhn? Oh I tells you, ef you aint got de milk en de dew of de old salvation when de long, cold years roll away!"

The use of the Bible, of the religious ceremony, then, helps to elevate these people who are chosen and distinguishes them from a Popeye or a Temple Drake. How much like the cry of a Hebrew prophet—say, Jeremiah—are these words of Dilsey: "I seed de beginnin, en now I sees de endin." In contrast to the materialist vision which is confined to the present, the elect have a *Weltanschauung* of past, present, and future. Stanley Cook's words about the ancient Hebrews can be applied here to Faulkner's own chosen people: "There was a feeling of corporateness and unity in space and in time: Yahweh's promises to the ancestors extend to their descendants; and for him to 'remember' Abraham, Isaac, and Jacob, or David, was to protect all Israel."[2]

We need not be overly shocked by the mention of incest in Faulkner's work—especially in *The Sound and the Fury*, *Sanctuary*, *Absalom, Absalom!* and "An Odor of Verbena"— and regard it as evidence of decadence. Incest has had a long history. In the Bible we have incestuous relationships in Genesis and II Samuel. It is clear that Lot's daughters sleep with him in an attempt to perpetuate his "seed." But the offspring are labeled as Moabites and the children of Ammon—they do not belong to the Hebrews, having been conceived in sin. In a similar way the incest between Ammon and his sister, Tamar, is condemned. Their brother, Absalom, becomes wrathful against Ammon for having forced Tamar to sleep with him; he eventually kills Ammon. This act of murder is "comforting" both to Absalom and to David. What do these two incidents indicate? I think they show that the "solidarity" of the Hebraic family unit was responsible for the closeness of the members—brother and sister, father and

[2] Stanley Cook, *An Introduction to the Bible* (Harmondsworth, England: Penguin Books, 1954), p. 89.

daughter. In an attempt to discourage the practice of in-breeding, the Hebrews developed severe penalties in regard to such carnal intercourse recorded especially in Leviticus and later in rabbinic codification and interpretation of marriage laws.

Faulkner's use of incest, then, is important because it brings up associations of a crime which has been tradition-ally condemned. This in turn adds to the legalistic tone of his work, implying that such people as Horace Benbow and Henry Sutpen are doomed. I don't think the incest motif is out of place, for Faulkner *is* concerned with the wholeness of the family unit. When Henry meets Bon, his stepbrother, in *Absalom, Absalom!* and takes him to his own home, where Bon finds Judith, a curious situation arises. The two brothers become attached to their sister. Of course this can be han-dled sensationally by an inferior writer, but Faulkner ex-plores the meaning of possible incest with subtlety. It is clear that Henry has not known any love from his father, Thomas Sutpen, who is dominated by his own abstractionism; Henry's dependence upon his sister has upheld him. Bon's arrival upon the family scene gives Henry an opportunity to express his need for affection in an unnatural manner. By means of this matchmaking between Bon and Judith, he is symboli-cally marrying her. Faulkner is saying that Henry not only wants to sleep with his sister—he wants to escape from the father-son conflict by changing into the bride, by becoming passive. This is, of course, the pattern which I have men-tioned in regard to Quentin Compson. And it leads to almost identical consequences: frustration and insanity.

In *Sanctuary* Horace Benbow, the lawyer, is obsessed, whether he realizes it or not, with the beauty of his step-daughter, Little Belle. He becomes conscious of his feelings only when he looks at her photograph. The reader can ask the reasons for this incest motif at the beginning of the novel. I think that Faulkner uses Horace's obsession symbolically, develops its implications when he meets Temple Drake. The lawyer begins to understand that Little Belle can be her *sis-ter*, that she has potentialities for being raped and corrupted by a Popeye. This is too simple. The association between the two girls in his mind, furthermore, demonstrates his am-bivalence: Horace does not completely condemn what has happened. Faulkner is saying that people such as this lawyer

are defeated by evil—as Benbow is when Goodwin is executed—because they have never understood their own inadequacies and frustrations. How can Horace save innocents if
he wants to sleep with his stepdaughter and Temple? This
is why he runs into the bathroom, after he has heard the
flapper's story and looked again at the photograph, to vomit.
It is his punishment.

Thus biblical themes influence Faulkner. I think, however, that he also uses the natural images of the Bible—the
flood, the animals, the flowers, to name a few. In "The Old
Man" section of *The Wild Palms*, Faulkner describes a Mississippi flood which engulfs much land and many inhabitants.
One of his most powerful pieces of writing, it shows the wildness of nature and the need of man to control the natural
forces. It is characteristic of Faulkner to think of the biblical Flood as he looks at this present-day catastrophe, and
through allusion to it he is able to make the convict and the
pregnant woman symbolic of Hebrews such as Noah who
were saved because of their holiness. The convict's fight to
help his companion (and later her child) becomes a universal
one. There is the same idea in *As I Lay Dying*, when the
Bundrens cross the river. As Darl and Jewel try desperately
to keep their mother's coffin from toppling, they are isolated
from the rest of the world. Water is all about them; they
alone can save Addie through concentrated, heroic efforts.
The violent situation becomes a symbol of cosmic proportions, of man's life, flooded by space and time.

Faulkner's description of animals results in his lengthy,
rhapsodic description of the mule in *Sartoris*. The extreme
care with which the animal is delineated is curious in this
early, family novel. Why does Faulkner stop to investigate
it? What accounts for the exaggeration of the description?
I believe we can assume that Faulkner—as he looked at the
mule—realized that there was a relationship between animals
that walk the earth and human beings. In his own mind he
came face to face not with rigidity of designs but with the
wildness of nature which, perhaps, must be tamed in a well-
ordered way. Faulkner learned the same kind of thing from
his observation of the mule in *Sartoris* that the writer of Job
did in looking at the leviathan: the need to comprehend as
completely as possible the wonder of all living things in spite
of an awareness of mortal weakness.

A few words about flowers. Like the Hebraic writers who characterized the "burning bush" out of which the Lord spoke to Moses, or the "fire of thorns" of their enemies (Psalm 118), Faulkner almost makes flowers come alive to influence the actions of men. No one can forget the voluptuous quality of honeysuckle which pervades Quentin's feelings about Caddy, his sister, or the faded wisteria of the South in *Absalom, Absalom!* Two scenes will demonstrate the violent nature of Faulkner's "burning" flowers. This passage from *Sanctuary*, describes Horace's incestuous feeling as he looks at the photograph before he vomits:

Communicated to the cardboard by some quality of the light or perhaps by some infinitesimal movement of his hands, his own breathing, the face appeared to breathe in his palms in a shallow bath of high light, beneath the slow, smoke-like tongues of invisible honeysuckle.

The second occurs in "An Odor of Verbena." Bayard smells the flower, verbena, after he returns to find his stepmother gone. He goes to his room and finds a single sprig which Drusilla has presumably left as a talisman on his pillow. The novel ends with the odor of the flower.

Obviously Faulkner has a wide understanding of the Old Testament. But I think it would be wrong to call him an orthodox believer because he has simply read and reread Hebraic literature. The Old Testament may supply traditional themes to his work, may lend its images to his work—Faulkner is, nevertheless, a modern writer. Actually he is trying to do the same thing that Joyce does in *Ulysses*. The very nature of Faulkner's parallelism of past and present is associated with his theme of order or—as in his major novels—the wrongness of rigidity as order. Perhaps the clearest indication I can make, in conclusion, is to say that the Hebrews believed in the omnipotence of a primitive but benevolent Yahweh. For Faulkner and many other contemporary writers and thinkers—Mann, James Joyce, or Freud—Yahweh has assumed new psychological attributes. In Faulkner's myth there are two behavioral principles continually at battle with each other—flexibility (good) and rigidity (evil). Unlike the Hebrews he believes that rigidity frequently wins.

FAULKNER AND
TWO PSYCHOANALYSTS

6

FAULKNER AND
TWO PSYCHOANALYSTS

Although I stressed the borrowings of Faulkner from the Bible in the last chapter, some mention should be made now of his relation to two psychoanalysts: Freud and Jung. It would be misleading to suggest that Faulkner has read and mastered the literature of these two men—in all probability he has not. I intend to show how a writer like Faulkner can arrive at the same kind of psychological truths as an analyst intent upon helping his patients.

The importance of Freud in Faulkner's work has been explained somewhat by Ruel Foster and others, who have discovered *Eros, Thanatos,* and the mechanics of dreams. But I believe that the major point of similarity has not yet been explored, that is, the Oedipal relationship, with the emphasis upon the struggle between the ego and the super-ego. To anyone with a knowledge of Freudian psychology, my discussion of the father-son relationship must remind him of such famous passages as these:

Psychoanalysis has revealed to us that the totem animal is really a substitute for the father, and this really explains the contradiction that it is usually forbidden to kill the totem animal, that the killing of it results in a holiday and that the animal is killed and yet mourned. The ambivalent emotional attitude which today still marks the father complex in our children and so often continues into adult life also extended to the father substitute of the totem animal.[1]

. . . . .

There is something fresh to be added: namely that in spite of everything the identification with the father finally makes a per-

[1] Sigmund Freud, *Totem and Taboo,* ed. A. A. Brill (London: George Routledge, 1919), p. 234.

manent place for itself in the ego. It is received into the ego, but establishes itself there as a separate agency in contrast to the rest of the content of the ego. We then give it the name of super-ego and ascribe to it, the inheritor of the parental influence, the most important functions. If the father was hard, violent and cruel, the super-ego takes over those attributed from him and, in the relations between the ego and it, the passivity which was supposed to have been repressed is reestablished. The super-ego has bcome sadistic, and the ego becomes masochistic; that is to say, at bottom passive in a feminine way. A great need for punishment develops in the ego, which in part offers itself as a victim to fate, and in part finds satisfaction in ill-treatment by the super-ego (that is, in the sense of guilt).[2]

.   .   .   .

Hence we know of two sources for feelings of guilt: that arising from the dread of authority and the later one from the dread of the super-ego.[3]

Obviously Freud's comments reveal many of the problems of Darl, Joe Christmas, Quentin, and Charles Bon. In Faulkner's myth these four sons are trying to discover the nature of their selves—they represent the ego, alone in the terrifying world. They are rebelling against their fathers, representatives of authority and, later, of the superego, who want to impose rigid patterns of behavior upon them. Faulkner's sons are ambivalent. They would like to submit, to accept things passively and gain a certain measure of security, but, at the same time, they realize that any individuality they may have is being crushed. Bon thinks about Sutpen, "*All right. I am trying to make myself into what I think he wants me to be; . . . I am young, young, because I still dont know what I am going to do.*" Quentin confesses to his father the incest which he can never commit. Darl fights to save Addie's coffin from toppling into the water, and yet he sets fire to the barn in a futile attempt to express his rebellion against her image. So they are doomed, being too weak to emerge victorious, desiring death as the last cruel form of punishment and peace from their fathers.

[2] Sigmund Freud, *Collected Papers*, ed. James Strachey (London: Hogarth Press, and Institute of Psycho-analysis, 1950), V, 231.

[3] Sigmund Freud, *Civilization and Its Discontents*, trans. Joan Riviere (London: Hogarth Press, and Institute of Psycho-analysis, 1953), p. 111.

This father-son, superego and ego, relationship appears even in a superficial book such as *The Unvanquished.* John Sartoris, rough and ready on his horse, embodies the authoritarianism of the father, the social conscience of the South. His motives are accepted unquestioningly by Drusilla and Rosa Millard, both more manly than womanly; however the son, Bayard, who, as a boy, wounded a Union soldier, tries to get at the heart of Sartoris. Of course he is guilt-ridden as he proclaims the deficiencies of the authority he has lived under for so long, and his final act of renunciation is quite courageous for this very reason. But Faulkner is able to make us feel that even *after* he refuses to avenge the murder of his father, which in part he unconsciously desired, Bayard is alone in a world he cannot understand. Freud also would believe this. The destructive qualities of childhood (the incidents of stealing mules, killing the grandmother's murderer, facing war) are not forgotten. It is difficult for the ego to find itself.

In the story "Barn Burning," Colonel Sartoris Snopes and his father, Ab, represent the same equation of ego and superego. Faulkner shows that the boy can lie in a courtroom to save his father from being called a "barn burner." The submission, however loyal it may be, cannot last because Colonel Sartoris Snopes learns about higher things than corruption: truth and justice. When Ab sets fire to another barn belonging to Major de Spain, the boy wants to fight back, to call his father evil. He cannot, for the same reason that Bayard cannot live happily after his failure to kill Redmond. In the story he runs away from the scene of Ab's corruption, from his "conscience," or so he thinks. Faulkner suggests that the flight of Colonel Sartoris Snopes is a chimera, that we, in turn, must discover the meaning of our relation to parental influence before we can call ourselves free.

The actual representative of authority is, perhaps, the character most frequently met in all of Faulkner's work. He influences not only the son but also the daughter. It would be repetitious to describe the relationships of Joanna Burden, Emily Grierson, Rosa Coldfield, and Drusilla to their fathers. They follow the identical pattern of the acceptance of the doctrine of their fathers and, consequently, they become "masculine," distrusting normal marriage. They find sexual outlets—Freud calls this process "sublimation"—in the affairs of men: war, social humanitarianism, concern with inflexible designs. In "Dr. Martino" Louise, a young, "epicene" (notice how often this word appears in Faulkner's descriptions) girl is attached to an old man who sits alone at a beach resort hotel, caring for him continually. Because of this relationship she cannot express herself sexually with Hubert Jerrod. There is dramatic power in the last scene. Louise *does* force herself to marry the young man (who is overwhelmed), after she rebels against old Dr. Martino and leaves him sitting alone before his last, fatal heart attack. I doubt that Hubert can ever replace the image of Dr. Martino for Louise, that he can be her equal in marriage.

In *The Psychoanalytic Theory of Neurosis*, Otto Fenichel, a Freudian disciple, writes the following passage about homosexuality, one of the consequences of the Oedipal relation of son to father:

Actually, "feminine" men often have not entirely given up their striving to be masculine. Unconsciously . . . they regard the condition of being a masculine man's "feminine" partner as learning the secrets of masculinity from the "master," or as depriving him of these secrets. In such cases the passive submission to the father is combined with traits of an old and original . . . identification love of the father. . . . Every boy loves his father as a model whom he would like to resemble; he feels himself the "pupil" who, by temporary passivity, can achieve the ability to be active later on. This type of love could be called the apprentice love; it is always ambivalent because its ultimate aim is to replace the master. After having given up the belief in his own impotence and having projected it onto the father, there are several ways in which a boy may try to regain participation in the father's omnipotence. The two opposite extremes are the idea of killing the father in order to take his place and the idea of ingratiation, of being obedient and submissive to such a degree that the father will willingly grant participation.[4]

There are some latent homosexual relationships in Faulkner's work—for instance, Quentin and Dalton Ames, Henry Sutpen and Charles Bon, Joe Christmas and McEachern, Darl and Jewel. Such relationships follow this striking pattern: the Faulknerian son, in the terms I have been using, ambivalent toward the towering father-image, learns to adopt a

[4] Otto Fenichel, *The Psychoanalytic Theory of Neurosis* (New York: W. W. Norton, 1945), p. 334.

passive attitude to the world about him. His relationship to another male (experienced, violent, or sophisticated, as in the case of Bon who is the "active" member of the alliance with Henry) can never be totally satisfactory. The passivity of the son compels him to be sexually attracted to the other man who becomes a father-surrogate. (This is what Freud calls "transference.") Afraid to yield to his hidden desires, he eventually expresses hostility. Quentin wants to attack Dalton who has slept with Caddy, his sister; Christmas, as we saw, enjoys McEachern's whipping and then beats him at the dance hall; Henry seduces Judith, his sister, because he has been "seduced" by Bon's worldliness, and he, of course, later murders Bon; Darl hates Jewel for being Addie's favorite, while his mind is filled with pictures of Jewel's physical activity, especially the beating of his horse. Can Faulkner mean that the son finally attacks the partner because he wants to destroy the father he has never really forgotten?

In his delineation of characters, particularly those influenced by the design, Faulkner suggests, in part, a dictum of Freud: psychological determinism. One example will suffice here. Faulkner is able to make us feel that for Quentin Compson, in *The Sound and the Fury*, life stopped in the past (the symbol is the broken watch). When he walks along with the little girl who has followed him, Quentin is repeating the relationship he once had with his sister, Caddy. In the past he tried to help her in awkward and immature ways— by striking Dalton Ames, her seducer, by proclaiming incest, and by trying to kill both of them. Now, he does not really know how to care for the playmate at his side, who thinks of him—as Caddy wanted to—as a big brother. The irony is quite apparent when he looks at her and says, almost unconsciously, "Come on, sister." Faulkner shows us, then, that Quentin cannot help this sister-image because he is only half-aware of things which are happening to him—he is repeating his childhood, as it were, in a compulsive manner. Consequently he cannot cope with the girl's brother who thinks that she has been kidnapped.

Although this element of psychological determinism exists in his work, I don't think Faulkner adheres to Freudian doctrine. He has more respect for the spiritual qualities of men. Freud's stress upon the importance of the Oedipus relationship as the starting point for all later activities, including belief in Christianity, ways of dreaming, even creating art, limits life. His theory is a dismal one, making us "anxious" to ask the following questions: Is Man to be reduced to a walking repetition compulsion? Is he basically the same today as he was when he was five years old? Don't present experiences influence behavior? In reply to these questions Freud would, I am sure, deny that existence is hopeless. The doubt remains for skeptical nonbelievers, however, that his doctrines *do* help to make the past somewhat of a permanent reality.

I have decided to show Faulkner's similarities to Jung because I believe that, despite his emphasis upon certain determinants, he is closer to what this psychoanalyst represents. Both men are concerned, in short, with the "individuation process," the psychological process that makes an individual of a human being. In his work Faulkner is trying to demonstrate that such "individuation" involves an ability to look clearly at past experience, the neurosis, if you will, so that it can become,

according to circumstance, the stimulus to the struggle for the wholeness of the personality, which is for Jung [and Faulkner] at once task and goal . . .—a goal independent of any medico-therapeutic viewpoint.[5]

Jung believes that this desire and need for self-realization, although especially significant in our times, has always existed. Indeed, it is responsible for the quantity of myths, legends, and fairy tales which deal with the hero of a quest— Jason, *Sir Gawain and the Green Knight*, Faust, to name a few. In his *Psychology of the Unconscious* Jung tries to show us the abundance of such quests which, even now, evoke wholehearted response, because, to use his own words,

. . . the myth of the hero . . . is . . . the myth of our own suffering unconscious, which has an unquenchable longing for all the deepest sources of our own being; for the body of the mother, and through it for her communion with infinite life in the countless forms of existence.[6]

[5] Jolan Jacobi, *The Psychology of Jung,* trans. K. W. Bash; Foreword by C. G. Jung (New Haven, Conn.: Yale University Press, 1953), p. 99.

[6] C. G. Jung, *Psychology of the Unconscious,* trans. Beatrice M. Hinkle (New York: Dodd, Mead, 1943), p. 231.

Of course there are finite ways of tracing this spiritual, psychological quest of the protagonist. Similar images reappear throughout the ages: search or hunt, confrontations with traditional beings, rebirth, the wheel of completion. Jung calls these images "archetypes." Faulkner's dependence upon such images does not mean simply that he has probably read Jung; the broad implication is that he, and the analyst, and all of us can recognize these "archetypes" because they are a fundamental part of human experience.

The hunt in Faulkner's novels is the ritualistic preparation for an understanding of individual standards of behavior which reject the rigidity of personal design. In the wilderness Isaac McCaslin learns from Sam Fathers, his spiritual guide, that he must leave the cold abstractionism of his region. He must remove his watch, his compass, and his gun because he is in the presence of natural fertility. He is not a white man any longer. Class distinctions are lost—he is merely the hunter out of time (the watch) and space (the compass). Isaac learns that Old Ben, the bear, is the symbol of the wildness of life which must be tamed in order to gain inner balance and serenity. He is hunted because he forces the hunter to use his own spirit to discover, to combat, and to defeat him. What Isaac is able to understand as the result of his hunt is that the individual cannot flee from the dangers he sees before him. He must engage in that "ancient and unremitting contest [of life] according to the ancient and unmitigable rules which voided all regrets and brooked no quarter. . . ." Nothing can help him except his own will. This is the reason he and Sam Fathers refuse to shoot Old Ben when they see him (and why Boon ambitiously attacks him to demonstrate that he *does* have physical strength). Ordering of the spirit or psyche is necessary—not killing.

Unfortunately, Faulkner realizes, the hunt to discover personal order is forgotten in our civilization. In his novels he believes that too many men chase instead of hunt; pursuit with ultimate destruction is their only motivation. In *The Sound and the Fury* Jason Compson, who represents the man of commerce, chases his fleeing niece in his car because she has stolen the money he embezzled from her mother. If he catches her he will feel that he has cornered a wild animal and proved his manhood. He never does, because he blacks out after inhaling the gas fumes from his speeding car. In

Light in August Percy Grimm chases Joe Christmas after the mulatto flees to the house of the Reverend Mr. Hightower. We see that Percy Grimm, who does capture his quarry, can gain satisfaction by making Joe as unmanned as he is. His sadism (like the whipping used by McEachern) is a type of perverse sexual expression which Krafft-Ebing could easily recognize. It demonstrates the fact that he—unlike Joe—has never had the desire to seek the significance of his manhood. Now looking again at *Sartoris* we can see the significance of Bayard Sartoris' destructive driving. In the same way as Grimm and Jason Compson, he can only feel a kind of exhilaration in movement toward eventual destruction. His car rides (and, of course, his airplane crash) are symbolic of man's need to prove himself not through internal order—as in Isaac's hunt—but through externalized speed. The chase enables Bayard to kill his own father, whose heart cannot withstand the reckless pace. The significance of the three chases, suggesting furious futility, is summarized, I believe, in the passages from *The Sound and the Fury* which stress the impotence of Jason at the end of his pursuit.

Jung has written that part of the "individuation process" involves closeness to the animal world. Primitive peoples frequently expressed their inner longing for fertility, bravery, immortality by means of transference to the great number of animate things about them: the horse, the cow, the fish. I will not attempt to point out the particular import of each animal because certain age-old associations are obvious—the cow, for instance, is a fertility symbol. Faulkner's use of animals is important in relating Man—even civilized, twentieth-century man—to the natural scene. He thus suggests man's need to return to nature by removal of some of his "instrumentalized" qualities. The following passages show the similarity of these animals, which are imbued with almost mystic significance, to the horse (and all animals) as a "libido" symbol in Jung's description.

In *Light in August* the horse is counterposed to the heifer. Christmas tries to ride McEachern's horse after he has attacked the Calvinist and escaped from the dance hall. He beats the animal, transferring his attack of the father-image to it, but as it refuses to respond to his violent commands, he abandons it. The incident is symbolic. He cannot make the horse do his bidding because he is not as powerful and masculine as the father. He cannot even assume the male role in his later sexual relationship to Miss Burden. In a related way the heifer is associated with the fecundity of the female. Christmas cannot bear to think that women are slaves to periodic filth after he learns about menstruation from his adolescent friends. He deliberately kills a heifer to discover the validity of this description. Christmas cannot accept the fact because of his own psychological constitution, which forces him to hate woman. These two incidents with their mythic suggestiveness reveal Joe Christmas' plight. On the objective level he cannot get close to the actual world of nature. On the symbolic level he cannot get close to either the male (the horse) or the female (the heifer).

In *As I Lay Dying* there is another use of the opposition of animals. The horse which Jewel owns is a symbol of wildness and "unnatural power" (as is the horse of Hightower's grandfather). He tries to tame the animal in an almost sexual way because he wants to assert his own power. Jewel can act like his horse and treat him with as much violence and ferocious contempt as he does the members of his family, especially Darl. Darl realizes that his brother's relationship to the horse parallels his relationship to Addie. Jewel, in a way, is rebelling against his treatment at the hands of his mother, who favored him more than any of her children and her husband. He is trying to assert his manhood before the eyes of Addie every time he maltreats the horse. He is, whether consciously or not, attacking rigidity through outbursts of power, which are purposeless except in a destructive way. Darl equates the horse with the mother in this poignant statement: "I cannot love my mother because I have no mother. Jewel's mother is a horse." Like his very sensitive brother, Vardaman is also conscious of the relationship between Addie and the animal world. On the day that Addie is ready to die, he brings home a fish which he caught in the stream. He begins then to associate the chopped fish with her. He seems to realize that the fish, long associated in the "collective unconscious" with fertility, is no longer alive. (His own mother is dead.) Actually the youngster is making a correspondence which Faulkner makes in the entire novel. Addie as dead fish means in a symbolic way that she is unfertile. Even though she has given birth to many children, she has not been able to love any, including Jewel. That she has not been a real mother to them is apparent in this seemingly incoherent passage from Vardaman's interior monologue:

> But my mother is a fish. Vernon seen it. He was there.
> "Jewel's mother is a horse," Darl said.
> "Then mine can be a fish, can't it, Darl?" I said.
> Jewel is my brother.
> "Then mine will have to be a horse, too," I said.
> "Why?" Darl said. "If pa is your pa, why does your ma have to be a horse just because Jewel's is?"
> "Why does it?" I said. "Why does it, Darl?"
> Darl is my brother.
> "Then what is your ma, Darl?" I said.
> "I haven't got ere one," Darl said. "Because if I had one, it is *was*. And if it is was, it can't be *is*. Can it?"
> "No," I said.
> "Then I am not," Darl said. "Am I?"
> "No," I said.

In *The Hamlet* we have the famous love affair between Ike Snopes, the idiot, and the cow. I think that although Faulkner ironically contrasts this "romance" to the story of Paris and Helen, he does want us to realize that Ike (almost a walking representation of the Freudian id) is different from the other materialistic members of the family, especially Flem, his brother. In his own fumbling way he is close to the natural scene; the cow symbolizes fecundity, and he, therefore, becomes associated in our minds with a kind of fertility which—although uncommon, to say the least—is nevertheless affirmative. (I may say that Ike Snopes' relationship to the cow means, in Jungian terms, a return to the "first mother," an "archetype" of peace, contentment, and security.) Faulkner uses hyperbole to stress his fondness for this isolated member of a shrewd, corrupt family.

Other "archetypes" of transformation for Jung are to be found in the four elements: earth, air, fire, water. Fire, for instance, signifies "emotional excitement or sudden bursts of impulse"[7] in the mythology of the complete process of self-realization. On the other hand, water signifies the mother's womb, birth (as in Jung's example of the god Mithra who, according to representations, was born beside a river),

---

[7] C. G. Jung, *Two Essays on Analytical Psychology*, trans. R. F. C. Hull (New York: Bollingen-Pantheon, 1953), p. 94.

and peace. Water can also represent the desire that death "might be the mother's womb,"[8] as in the Jonah story. Of course Faulkner does not choose the four elements deliberately, but it is clear that they, like his animals, account for the primitivism in his work, and they suggest the need to return to primary sources of experience as an antidote for man's "dissociation of sensibility." Faulkner's work emphasizes all four elements: fire in *The Sound and the Fury, As I Lay Dying, Absalom, Absalom!* and *A Fable*; air in *Pylon* and "Death Drag"; earth in "The Bear," "Red Leaves," *The Hamlet*, and *Requiem for a Nun*; water in *The Wild Palms, As I Lay Dying, Intruder in the Dust,* and *The Sound and the Fury*.

In *Intruder in the Dust* baptism is an important ritual, illustrating water symbolism. I have already emphasized that Charles Mallison Jr.'s descent into the ice pond is the first time he begins to associate himself meaningfully with Lucas Beauchamp. He is aware that he and the Negro share a ritualistic bond which cannot be broken in spite of Charles' resistance. In the novel he has to comprehend, however, the *total* meaning of this experience. This ritual which symbolizes the beginning of a new learning process occurs in a different context in *The Sound and the Fury*. Caddy loses her virginity to Dalton Ames, and she realizes after this that she carries the taint of sin, at least in the eyes of Quentin and Benjy, her idiot brother. Benjy—with his uncanny sensitivity—senses the loss of his sister's virginity and communicates his disgust to her. Caddy feels frantically that she has to cleanse herself. She runs to the bathroom sink. Then she tries to throw herself into the stream near the Compson house. Quentin's suicide occurs in this novel. Early on his last day at Harvard, he walks past a lake where some boys are swimming. He remembers past experiences which are connected in his mind with water—especially the incident in which he and his sister discussed incest after her attempted immersion. Quentin believes, after looking at the water, that he can forget his internal torments only if he kills himself. Perhaps death by water, the Jonah motive, can be a baptism for him. He thinks, "And I will look down and see my murmuring bones and the deep water like wind, like a roof of

---

[8] C. G. Jung, *Psychology of the Unconscious*, p. 245.

wind, and after a long time they cannot distinguish even bones upon the lonely and inviolate sand."

The use of opposites in Faulkner's work, especially in *Light in August*, has already been cited in Chapter 4. Both Faulkner and Jung believe that man can learn the nature of his own psyche by use of an opposing principle. In the "individuation process," Jung is convinced, the hero in quest of his identity frequently meets beings who embody certain principles. Some of these beings are the Shadow, who symbolizes our other aspect (a good example is Dostoyevsky's *Double*), the Soul-Image, a symbol of "the respective contrasexual portion of the psyche,"[9] the Old Wise Man, "the personification of the spiritual principle"[10] in the male, and *Magna Mater*, the great earth-mother. Some of these "archetypes" are in Faulkner:

Shadow. The meeting of father and son in Faulkner is symbolic of the confrontation with the other aspect: Hightower–Christmas, the General–the Corporal, Mr. Compson–Quentin. Of course these meetings involve more destruction than learning.

Soul-Image. The meeting of Byron and Lena or of the convict and the pregnant woman is a positive occurrence. Faulkner's men seem to learn less than the women about the contrasexual portion of their psyches.

Old Wise Man. Lucas Beauchamp, Sam Fathers, and Gavin Stevens embody the "spiritual principle" adopted by youths in search of their manhood.

Magna Mater. Lena Grove, the pregnant woman in "The Old Man," and even corrupt Dewey Dell represent matter in the female as opposed to the "spiritual principle" in the male. Faulkner does not allow a masculine woman such as Emily Grierson to meet *Magna Mater* and thus to learn about her residual femininity.

It is evident that Faulkner has used these "archetypes" in his novels; furthermore, like Jung, he realizes that most people can never become whole units. They cannot discover the meaning of these confrontations with different phases of humanity or with their own natures. The road to complete "individuation" is difficult and only a few (perhaps they

---

[9] Jacobi, *The Psychology of Jung*, p. 104.
[10] *Ibid.*, p. 115.

should be called the "self-chosen") reach the end of it: Isaac, Sam Fathers, the Corporal, Dilsey, Gavin Stevens.

Jung writes, in contrast to Freud, that the wholeness of time is significant in the development of the person. His dream interpretation stresses events which occur after childhood traumas and, indeed, in the immediate present. (Many middle-aged patients have come to him for treatment because of this very emphasis upon growth.) Freud stresses the importance of the number three—the id, the ego, the superego; the Oedipal triangle—whereas Jung stresses the number four. He finds it in the basic psychological functions, the four elements; and historical examples such as the Pythagorean tetractys and the mandalas. Jolan Jacobi, author of an introductory study of Jung, says:

The unique symbolism of the mandalas exhibits everywhere the same rules and regularity of arrangement: namely, the reference of the elements, arranged in a circle or square, to a center, by which "wholeness" is meant to be symbolized. Many of them have the form of a flower, cross, or wheel, with a manifest inclination to the number four.[11]

Unlike Freud, Jung does not dare to stop time in the first years of life because he, himself, is searching for completion in life.

Some isolated images of fulfillment are found in Faulkner's work. The number four is important in *The Sound and the Fury*, with its four sections, arranged to give meaningful order. Benjy, at the end when he howls, and Dilsey both experience certain kinds of completion ("I seed de first en de last"). The wheel is important in *Light in August*. Lena at the beginning and at the end goes along the road of life, sure of her destination, "satisfied." In "The Bear" Ike has a vision of past-present-future as he looks at Sam Fathers' grave. The quotation from Keats' "Ode on a Grecian Urn" in Part Four emphasizes timelessness. In *The Wild Palms* the convict, caught in the Mississippi flood, forgets about his life sentence and with determination battles the troubles which now beset him. Like Eliot's use of fourness in *Four Quartets*, or Mann's description of time's well in *Joseph*, or Proust's recovery of the past, Faulkner's symbols suggest the necessity of living cyclically or fully.

[11] *Ibid.*, p. 128.

Faulkner tries to concern himself with the number four, the wheel, the still point, in short, with the wholeness of life. In this passage from *Requiem for a Nun* Faulkner tries to capture the frozen moment, the still point, in which all of time is held in the present. A contemporary visitor is looking at a scratch on a window made by a girl who waited in vain for her lover to return from war. This is a good illustration of Faulkner—like Jung, the psychoanalyst—*imploring* us to become "I's" in this age of rigidity. The passage is the essence of wisdom we would do well to remember: to make a heroic effort to leave a mark in life:

. . . she [the girl]was—not *might* have been, nor even *could* have been, but *was*: so vast, so limitless in capacity is man's imagination to disperse and burn away the rubble-dress of fact and probability, leaving only truth and dream—then gone, you [the visitor] are outside again, in the hot noon sun: . . . to unfumble among the road signs and filling stations to get back onto a highway you know, back into the United States; not that it matters, since you know again now that there is no time: no space: no distance: a fragile and workless scratching almost depthless in a sheet of old barely transparent glass, and . . . there is the clear undistanced voice as though out of the delicate antenna—skeins of radio, further than empress's throne, than splendid insatiation, even than matriarch's peaceful rocking chair, across the vast instantaneous intervention, from the long long time ago: *'Listen stranger; this was myself: this was I.'*

CONCLUSION

CONCLUSION

Throughout this book I have tried to emphasize that Faulkner is concerned with the fictional representation of the father-son relationship. Not much is known about Faulkner's own parents. However, Robert Coughlan, in his *Life* articles, has hinted at the relative inadequacies of Murry, Faulkner's father, at the time he fought with a druggist named Walker after the latter had made a remark about Murry's sister. Murry, it seems, was unable to display any strength (he was hit in the mouth by Walker's shots but was not killed), and the family decided to move from Ripley to Oxford, Mississippi, because of this and other violent incidents. I think the incident should be related to those involving Faulkner's great-grandfather, Colonel William. We know more about him than we do about the parents. This, in itself, is a significant fact. The Colonel was a man of huge proportions: he fought in the War, constructed a railroad, wrote a novel in 1860, *The White Rose of Memphis*, bowled, on the alley he had set up in his front yard, after working past midnight. He captured the imagination of his descendants, particularly of his namesake, William Faulkner, who was later to say to his young classmates that he wanted to be a writer like Colonel William.

Growing up in the small town of Oxford, Faulkner was sure to hear tales about this heroic figure and to regard him as most children regard George Washington. I believe that he became "obsessed"—one of his favorite words—to the point of idol-worship, probably at the expense of his father Murry. If he had stopped here, we would have only novels such as *The Unvanquished*. But Faulkner became aware, as he developed, that his great-grandfather had flaws. The inhumanity of slavery, as well as the unscrupulous competing with business partners, became associated in his mind with the distant Colonel. How am I to judge what my great-grandfather represents? Is Colonel William good or evil? Should I be the same kind of man when I mature? Faulkner faced these questions and could not resolve them. They plagued him and made him feel guilt-ridden. It is, therefore, appropriate that his first two, inferior novels, *Soldiers' Pay* and *Mosquitoes*, did not deal with the father-son relationship. Faulkner, as we know, did not continue to flee from the answers to the moral questions of his past. In his five great novels, *The Sound and the Fury*, *As I Lay Dying*, *Light in August*, *Absalom, Absalom!* and *A Fable*, he is true to his muse: he grapples with the problems posed by his relation to Colonel William.

Light in August is one example. Richard Chase believes that "in the case of Hightower there seems to be a failure of consciousness precisely at that point where we should understand the association between him and his own history."[1] Chase's doubts imply that this failure, which I don't believe exists, mirrors the ambivalence of Faulkner's mind. I believe that Faulkner is closer to Hightower than to any other character in the novel. Hightower seems to be the spokesman for his creator when he thinks about the destruction Calvinism can bring. He states the theme when he hears about the murder committed by Joe, and his statement that Christmas' plight is symbolic of man's plight is an outburst Faulkner makes throughout *Light in August*. But this is not all. The grand conception of the grandfather with which Hightower is obsessed is akin to the grand conception of Thomas Sutpen and John Sartoris, and, of course, to that of Colonel William. (It is significant that Hightower remembers the galloping hooves of his ancestor's horse; we can remember the comments of Wash Jones as he looks at Sutpen on his horse.) The correspondence between Faulkner and Hightower shows us the writer's approach to the psychological conflict which is at the source of his art. He is close to the design of the father in *Light in August* because his consciousness broods about the weakness and decay of contemporary Southerners; mechanical trends disgust him. The very facts of his birth in Mississippi and his relationship to Colonel William force him to be aware of the constructive values of the past, the glory of the ante-bellum aristocracy, and this awareness is in conflict with commercial parasitism, the absence of moral and psychological strength, which he sees as dangers in this age.

[1] Richard Chase, "The Stone and the Crucifixion: Faulkner's *Light in August*," in *William Faulkner: Two Decades of Criticism*, p. 215.

The design of the denial of life, however, is not the solution to his confusion and his need for order. Faulkner is different from Hightower because he chooses to remain in the midst of present conditions, horrible as they are.

This is not easy. Faulkner returns repeatedly to Colonel William in a desperate attempt to grasp his meaning. Consequently Faulkner creates a father who is both authoritarian and loving, good and evil, in his great novels. We have seen that Sutpen, Addie Bundren, Hightower torment sons trying to discover their fathers' reasons for behaving as rigidly as they do. Quentin kills himself because of his inability to comprehend Mr. Compson's pessimism. Darl becomes a lunatic who wants to preserve *and* destroy his parent's image. Both mulattoes, Joe Christmas and Charles Bon, admire the power of their white fathers, but they attack that power as it begins to crush them. The same pattern of confusion, of guilt over opposing views toward the father, of futile rebellion, is shown in these four sons, and it forces them to action. For me the Corporal in *A Fable* is a freak despite his noble purpose. His judgments about what is happening to him come too swiftly; he is too sure of himself in the midst of military violence. Faulkner is probably able to breathe more life into the four sons than into the Corporal because he is facing with honesty his personal relation to his great-grandfather. There is more of Christ than Faulkner in the Corporal, and, ironically, the writer knows his distraught self better than he does the sacrificial lamb.

Many people have called Faulkner decadent because he has presented the consequences of an unusual father-son relationship: obsession and homosexuality among them. I have tried to indicate a failure of Faulkner to portray women and "normal" marriage adequately. His childhood "attraction" toward Colonel William, in all likelihood, retarded his desire to concern himself with feminine women. In Faulkner's novels, we enter a world where fathers and sons are so interested in conflicts of will, with sexual overtones, that they disregard or fear emotions for healthy women. Faulkner specializes in twisted creatures such as Temple Drake and Joanna Burden and Miss Habersham, who are willful and masculine. Who is to blame for this strange kind of person—man or woman? I think it is quite evident that Faulkner condemns women harshly for being masculine, but he never gives them the chance to flower into femininity. It is not enough to demonstrate Faulkner's brutal treatment of sex— it is more to the point to regard his treatment as latently homosexual or, if this is too extreme, Oedipal.

No one can read Faulkner without noting the abundance of obsessive-compulsive behavior. Hightower, Sutpen, and Popeye are all compulsives, fleeing from the outside world so they can achieve peace and security. Christmas, Quentin, and Colonel Sartoris Snopes are compulsives, trying to escape from their fathers' influence, proclaiming their individuality constantly to themselves and to everyone about them. And above these compulsive actions of fathers and sons hovers Faulkner. He too is attached to the problems involved; he too is seeking an explanation of the meaning of obsession. Thus similar images reappear: flight from and hunt for objects. There are the flights of Christmas and the convict in "The Old Man" away from responsibility to women, the attempts of Quentin to elude his shadow on June 2, 1910, the retreat of Henry Sutpen from Sutpen's Hundred, with his new-found friend, Charles Bon (and his eventual return). There is the hunt for objects. Christmas tries to find recognition at Hightower's house; Quentin attacks Dalton Ames, his sister's seducer; Boon grasps for squirrels; Jewel Bundren attacks his horse. Risking a generalization, I would say that Faulkner's emphasis upon obsessive-compulsive behavior and on the polarities of flight and hunt, retreat and attack, represent a mind in unstable equilibrium. Faulkner shows us that he is unsure in handling his own psychological problems. He does not know whether to flee from his dilemma or to attack it head on. At last he *wills* himself to stand in perilous balance, and as a result, he produces novels such as *Light in August*. I emphasize again the uncertainty about Colonel William and, symbolically, the past (childhood, the ante-bellum South, Eden) to indicate that Faulkner's art is produced by and in strife. This explains its tension, contemporary relevance, and, I think, universality.

I believe Faulkner has seen the essentially mythic qualities of his life in his art. He can liken his sons to Biblical sons, believing that they have similar problems. Bon becomes, in our minds, a greater person than he is—an Absalom. Faulkner can connect Gavin Stevens' idea about social progress with the Old Testament covenant because he knows that human actions involve the fundamentals of love and patience and are timeless. This use of traditionalism rescues his five novels from the slough of possible self-indulgence and puts them into dramatic and lasting fiction. The point is well illustrated by contrasting *The Hamlet* and most of Mark Twain's fiction. When we read about the cub striking out at Mr. Brown in *Life on the Mississippi*, or the demonic attractiveness of Philip Traum, we feel that curious, unimportant things have taken place, that Twain has not explored, merely sentimentalized, the reactions of his characters. Mark Twain does not think of them as timeless—simply as hazy participants in an unreal world which, at times, is especially funny. *The Hamlet* is as good an example of frontier literary tradition as any of Twain's works. It assumes greater proportions through mythological reference. Eula is more Cymbele than a voluptuous girl; Ike's cow is undefiled Fertility; the hound which follows Mink is brutal, primitive Justice; the Snopes are Evil. Faulkner is, in many ways, just as funny as Twain (especially in the incident of the spotted horses), but he is also aware of traditional associations in his treatment not only of animals and elements but of people. Thus Faulkner's art is greater because he sees more than himself.

Faulkner directs attention to what I consider one of the recurring themes of American literature: the son, in search of a spiritual father, trying to learn about himself and his relationship to society and to the world at large. I find this theme not only in Twain's *Pudd'nhead Wilson*, but also in Melville's "Billy Budd," Franklin's *Autobiography*, and Capote's *Other Voices, Other Rooms*. Melville explores the conflict between primitive individuality and legalistic authority in "Billy Budd." Like Faulkner he employs the father-son relationship, comparing the closeness of Captain Vere and Billy to that of Abraham and Isaac as Billy is sacrificed to the Captain's law. Melville hints at sociopolitical implications. Free Billy represents the new American independence, which is doomed because it confronts European social restraints too late. Melville believes, however, that Billy realizes the importance of experience and of the assumption of responsibilities in the world. *Pudd'nhead Wilson* is a cruel book, describing the rebellion of Tom, a part-black scoundrel, against his authoritarian mother (an Addie Bundren). Roxy, his mother, is a Calvinist because she tries to make her son conform to the standards of those who are saved. She molds Tom from birth to make him "white" (good), and her excessive devotion to this course of action is largely responsible for his later rebelliousness. Like a Faulknerian son, Tom emerges as a man destroyed by the design. Capote is less complex than Twain, Melville, or Faulkner. He does show us, nevertheless, his decadent concern with perversion. Joel Harrison Knox in *Other Voices, Other Rooms* is as doomed as Billy or Tom or Christmas—his doom is overt homosexuality. Capote's father-representative in the novel is Cousin Randolph, a homosexual intent upon the young boy's seduction. Joel, isolated in Noon City, is powerless (more weak-willed than any of the aforementioned sons) to resist the other's advances, and he falls hard. Faulkner's use of the father-son relationship, then, relates him to American myth. Perhaps it is his insistence upon probing his own heritage and that of our guilt-ridden society which made him an outcast until 1945. Since then he has begun to assume gradually an air of respectability in the public eye, presumably because his later novels deal with justice, spiritual suffering, and salvation. Faulkner surely deserves this recognition as more than a white supremist. I believe, however, that the recognition for his treatment of the tortured father-son relationship, with its implications of maturation, will be more lasting than this superficial recognition as expressed in *Life* and *Time*. Such recognition does not do justice to his analysis of the American consciousness. For Faulkner, the prodigal son does not return joyously. His son searches for new meaning in life, meaning which is frequently at odds with his environment. Faulkner's son—the symbol of contemporary America—who rebels against the abstract authoritarian pattern of the past and the present, is doomed unless he can gain the respect of his neighbors.

But returning to Faulkner's criticism, I believe that his father-son relationship has been neglected. In the past the inability to understand the importance of this relationship has been responsible for some of the following critical errors: (1) *As I Lay Dying* concerns the "poor whites," so instead of looking at Addie and Darl, critics investigated the novel as they would a sociology text. (2) *Light in August* was considered by many to be a fragment, rather than a unified work dealing with one son and five fathers. (3) *Absalom,*

Absalom! received a disproportionate amount of attention as a work containing the key to Faulkner's psychology, instead of just one aspect of it. (4) *A Fable* was reviewed by many critics as an isolated novel. It is, however, closely connected with the Yoknapatawpha County novels in its delineation of the father-son conflict. (5) In general, Faulkner's novels were considered either tracts or historical documents, limited to the South. I have tried to show that they contain traditionalism, contemporary psychology, and a recurring theme of American literature.

If we realize that Faulkner has transformed his own relationship to Colonel William into five relationships in his great novels, we can see the fertility of his imagination. Glancing at these five novels, I see a connecting line from Mr. Compson–Quentin, to Addie–Darl, to Hightower–Christmas, to Sutpen–Bon, to the General–Corporal. It is very clear that Faulkner's treatment of the relationship has developed from the simple, limited conflict of Compson, to the more complex struggle of Bon and Christmas against entire societies, and finally to the cosmic struggle of the two "military" men. Curiously Faulkner's own ambivalence toward the distant Colonel makes his fathers and sons complex beings who act in subtle ways, which they can only understand individually. This reinforces the feeling of the separation of generations. For me the attack of and retreat from his complex great-grandfather is responsible for Faulkner's wonderfully intricate portrayal of Thomas Sutpen, the archetype of his fathers in the entire mythology.

William Faulkner does not want his conflicts to be charted or his greatness to be extolled. He asks that we read his novels with comprehension of the curse of the authoritarian design, embodied in the misunderstanding between father and son, that we reread such descriptions as the one of Hightower, thinking not only of Christ but of *every* crucified son:

'And they will do it gladly,' he says, in the dark window. He feels his mouth and jaw muscles tauten with something premonitory, something more terrible than laughing even. 'Since to pity him would be to admit selfdoubt and to hope for and need pity themselves. They will do it gladly, gladly. That's why it is so terrible, terrible, terrible.'

INDEX